# PRAISE FOR
## *The Right Problems: What the President, Congress, and Every Candidate Should Be Working On*

"I devoted my life to fighting racial injustice. The Right Problems defines the template for fighting the injustices we have all endured, namely, a dysfunctional federal government. We must solve these problems now!"
**Roy Innis, Chairman, Congress of Racial Equality (CORE)**

"This book clearly identifies *The Right Problems* and priorities we ought to be working on in Congress for our nation. As a first term Senator I now see why it is so difficult to accomplish the solutions presented here, which I am determined to help achieve. Thank you my brother (Herman Cain) from another mother!
**Senator David Perdue (R-GA)**

"The common-sense solutions presented in this book are spot on. Our job in Congress is to garner the will and support to make them happen. We must not leave the bill and failures of this out-of-control federal government to our grandchildren. My friend Herman Cain adds appreciable clarity to ways in which we can correct the very dangerous path we are on"
**Congressman Tom Price, M.D. (R-GA)**

"My uncle, MLK once said that the American dream reminds us that every person is an heir of the legacy of dignity and worth. Herman Cain embodies this legacy and brings it home with common sense solutions to America's problems."

**Dr. Alveda King, author and civil rights activist**

"Mr. Cain's legion of fans that know him will thoughtfully nod while they read this book, as they have come to know his grasp of this nation's painful problems. Those new to his message will be encouraged with the clarity and achievability of the solutions."

**Timothy P. Taft, CEO and President – Fiesta Restaurant Group, Inc.**

"It is my sincere hope that a groundswell of concerned patriots will pay close attention to the poignant insight provided by Herman Cain in the 'The Right Problems.' Our nation is facing real problems, and the commonsense solutions Herman provides are second-to-none. I thank God for Herman Cain and for his bold ideas that are so badly needed in Washington D.C. If we can stay focused and address the right problems, we can see America's greatness restored...and this book will prove to be an essential starting place!"

**Congressman Jody Hice, (R-GA)**

"I like predictable men -- when they're predictably right. Herman Cain is such a man who has accomplished so much: businessman, public policy leader, communicator, presidential candidate. With "The Right Problems" he now adds polemicist to the list. He tackles our nation's problems boldly, seriously and confidently -- as only Herman Cain can. Liberals don't want you to read this book, which is why you should."

**Brent Bozell, Founder and President of**
**Media Research Center**

"If we are going to start creating more businesses than are closing again, then these are 'The Right Problems' and solutions to be working on. This is badly needed common sense."

**Jim Clifton, Chairman and CEO of Gallup**

"With the pragmatism, optimism, and humor that have made him a business and media success, Herman Cain serves up a slice of much-needed common sense in *The Right Problems*. Whether you're aiming for the White House or the corner office, you'll find Herman's clear-eyed method of identifying and attacking fundamental issues indispensable."

**Jon Klein, Co-Founder and CEO, TAPP TV**

# THE RIGHT PROBLEMS

### WHAT THE **PRESIDENT, CONGRESS,** AND EVERY **CANDIDATE** SHOULD BE WORKING ON

*NEW YORK TIMES* BESTSELLING AUTHOR

## HERMAN CAIN

A POST HILL PRESS BOOK
ISBN (hardback): 978-1-68261-008-4
ISBN (eBook): 978-1-68261-009-1

THE RIGHT PROBLEMS
What the President, Congress, and Every Candidate Should Be Working On
© 2016 by Herman Cain
All Rights Reserved
Cover Design by Quincy Alivio
Cover Photo of Herman Cain by Darrell Emory

**Post Hill**

PRESS

Post Hill Press
275 Madison Avenue, 14th Floor
New York, NY 10016
http://posthillpress.com

*To my wife, Gloria, of 48 years!*
*and*
*ALL Grandchildren who will inherit a national*
*mess if we don't fix it.*

# CONTENTS

# FOREWORD

Herman Cain's *The Right Problems* is a serious book that every American should read before voting in 2016.

America today faces challenges on many fronts. As Herman points out, it is we the people who must take the lead in forcing our elected officials to confront these important problems.

Herman understands that the center of responsibility in a free society is the citizens, not the politicians. It is citizens who bear the ultimate responsibility for their country's future.

This civic obligation is especially strong in America, where our founding document, the Declaration of

Independence, says that each of us is "endowed by our Creator with certain unalienable rights." That principle asserts a grant of sovereignty from God to the citizen, not of power to the government. It is the key to explaining why the American Revolution was so startling to those who were comfortable with kings and dictators.

Because Herman understands the citizen's role in America, he has outlined a citizen-based vision to turn America around.

He came to these ideas through years of hard work in business, politics and radio.

Indeed, Herman is a remarkable leader and citizen. When he was the successful CEO of Godfather's Pizza, I asked him as speaker to play a leading role in revising the tax code on the Kemp Commission. He also played an important role at the Federal Reserve Bank of Kansas City.

After his business career, Herman became a very popular talk radio host. He turned that following into a launching pad for a presidential campaign. Many of the most exciting ideas in the 2012 presidential contest came from Herman Cain.

The Cain for President campaign was filled with new thinking and at times dominated the nominating process with its creative solutions to America's problems

Now he has taken three years to consider the challenges we face as Americans. Herman has returned to talk radio, where he continues to listen to everyday Americans who call in with their insights and comments. This grassroots connection gives Herman a very different perspective than you hear from Washington think tanks and lobbyists.

Herman understands that the key challenges are very different than the often trivial issues that can dominate the daily news.

With *The Right Problems*, Herman Cain offers a much more substantive vision of what the 2016 campaign should be about. Read it, and then get involved to turn it into a reality. That is what citizens in a free society do.

—Newt Gingrich, former Speaker of the
U.S. House of Representatives

# INTRODUCTION

Are you as sick and tired as I am of politicians focusing on "what's do-able" instead of fixing the problems? As a result, we have made no progress on reducing the national debt, balancing the federal budget, reducing the size of government, replacing the tax code, restructuring Social Security and Medicare/Medicaid, maintaining a "peace through strength" military, or pushing back the threat of radical Islamic terrorists who want to kill all of us!

The political establishment (the president, members of Congress and the political consultant class) just assume these issues are not doable so they don't try. It's called lack of leadership, courage, and integrity. And if someone does suggest a solution instead of another political band-aid, the mainstream media (MSM) is there to demagogue the solution until it kills it, or falsely discredits the champion of the solution. Or, people just stop talking about it.

The not do-able attitude will not change until we have a real leader (Chapter Five) in the White House with courage and integrity, as well as massive public pressure from the people by way of Article V of the Constitution (Chapter Seven)—one solution at a time! Politicians hate this approach because it changes their power over the people to the power of the people.

Real solutions in Washington D.C. never survive because of partisan politics and an electorate which is easily deceived and manipulated. Too many people do not take the time to become "informed" because, in fairness, they are just trying to survive day to day.

As a result, they depend upon the spoon-fed sound bites of the MSM and professional politicians (those that have been in office w-a-a-y too long) for their information. Most of the people are not stupid, they're just misinformed, uninformed, or confused, but assumed to be stupid by the elected class who thinks they are the ruling class. Can we say "Gruber-gate"?

Therefore, the rest of us will have to save the savable and save the United States of America. I believe it's doable!

So let's get started.

"Them that's going get on the wagon; them that ain't get out of the way."

# CHAPTER 1

## DON'T BE IGNORANT

### An Informed Public Pressures Elected Officials to Work on the Right Problems

I've read some of the funniest theories about why I ran for president in the 2012 cycle. The funniest is that I ran for president so I could make a lot of money selling books about it afterward. Anyone who believes that one should try running for president— and find out what happens when you rack up campaign debt for which you are personally responsible at the conclusion of your campaign.

I had a lot more money before I ran for president than after. If I did it as a business decision, it was one of my worst.

Of course, that's not why I did it at all. Ironically, I ran for president because I believe my track record of making actual business decisions is a pretty good one. I thought I could be a good president because, when I looked at the Obama administration and how it made decisions, I realized that they had no practical concept for how to identify a crucial problem and solve it.

And in my years in business, that is what I excelled at. I certainly understood that I was an unconventional candidate, and that I didn't act the way political consultants try to make candidates act (nor did I ever intend to), but I figured if I had a shot it was to catch fire with some really interesting ideas, then ride those ideas along with strong debate performances to the latter stages of the nomination race. The one idea that really got attention, of course, was the

9-9-9 tax plan. So up to that point we made the strategy work pretty well.

Obviously I didn't make it because of the false accusations made against me that brought my campaign to an end, so the strategy didn't ultimately succeed. (By the way, I thoroughly took those accusations apart on HermanCain.com some time back. Go there and search for "truth wins" if you haven't seen it. I don't intend to go back into that in this book.)

So I didn't become president, and today I'm happy hosting my radio show, giving speeches and generally enjoying life with my wife and my family. I'm not afraid to try things and fail, and when people refer to me as a "failed presidential candidate," all that means is that I gave it a shot.

But the reason I ran for president is still pertinent today. If I had to cite one lesson as the most important thing I've learned during my business career— whether at Pillsbury, Burger King, Godfather's Pizza or even now with my company T.H.E. New Voice— it's that it's not enough just to know how to work on problems. What you have to be able to do is work on the right problems.

This seems simple enough, but it escapes many people— and many whole organizations.

Sometimes these are called leverage points, but I don't want to devolve into a lot of business-speak in this book. Basically we're talking about the problems that have the greatest impact on an organization as a whole. It takes some doing to identify what these are. You might think it's obvious, but proving that requires the ability to understand how the organization works as a whole, and to be able to explain why solving a given problem also improves your performance in 10, or 50, or 1,000 other areas.

A lot of organizations focus on lower-leverage problems for a variety of reasons. One is that they're easier. You've heard of dealing first with the "low-hanging fruit," which means you start by taking care of things you can tackle quickly. There's something to that, but only if the low-hanging fruit helps lead you to the real high-leverage issues. Otherwise you're getting things done but not making much difference.

Another reason organizations sometimes fixate on the wrong problems is that someone, or a group of someones, has an agenda that revolves around those issues. Corporate politics can be as counterproductive as real politics, and if it pleases a certain person or persons to keep people busy in a given area, then that's where people will be busy.

Of course, one of the biggest reasons organizations work on the wrong problems is that people can't agree what the right problems are— and those in leadership either don't recognize the right problems themselves or aren't willing to tell everyone else what to focus on.

When I took over Godfather's Pizza, I realized immediately that we had to focus on our service and our product quality. Service had gotten off track because people either didn't care or they did not understand its critical importance. Product quality had gotten off track because restaurant operations had gotten away from some of the standards for ingredients specifications, and inconsistencies in just making the pizza right.

Service and quality became our primary focus. Those were the right problems! We updated all standards, specifications and procedures and drove the message throughout the company like a laser on steroids. It worked, and customers started to come back more often. Of course we had to also make some marketing and promotional changes to get them to the restaurants, but service and quality brought them back.

I'm not trying to tell you I was some sort of genius CEO. I just knew the right question to ask, which was, of all the problems we're dealing with, which one makes the most difference?

### *What are the right problems to work on?*

I believe our country is in trouble right now because we have not had leaders working on the right problems for a very long time. Solving that is a multifaceted challenge, but it starts with understanding how the political process is different from the running of a business. A CEO can look at the numbers and examine the operation of a company, and make a determination of what the right problems are—then act to solve those problems.

In government, before you even have a leader in place, the public has to make a collective decision about what type of person it wants as a leader. And that decision is going to be heavily influenced by the problems the public thinks are most important.

That leads to a difficult but important question that we can't be afraid to ask: Does the public really know what the right problems are? And if not, why not?

I think very highly of the American public, but I am going to give you a candid answer to the question. I don't think the public knows what the right problems are, because the public is either uninformed or ill-informed. That leads to the election of leaders who either don't know the right problems to work on or see no need to figure it out, because the public isn't clamoring for them to do so.

So it stands to reason that if the public was better informed, we would have more of a public consensus about what the right problems are— and what they are not. To a large degree, the public is ill-informed because the news media (which also do not know the right problems we should be working on) do its jobs poorly— we'll get into that soon enough in this book. But there are simple things the public can do that can make them better informed and better able to assess the right problems our leaders should be working on.

First, people need to keep the value of media reporting in perspective. The media are selective in what they report, partly because they have no choice. Time and available resources limit them and force them to make decisions about what can receive their attention. But also realize: They often don't make very good decisions. They don't focus on the right issues and the right problems often enough, either because they don't recognize the problems, or because it's easier to focus on something else, or because they just don't want to.

Consider how much time the media will often spend on the search for a missing plane, or the emerging details of a natural disaster, or the criminal trial of a celebrity that would garner no news coverage at all if the accused was an average citizen. You can argue the news value of any such story, but one thing you can't deny is that these stories take away from the limited time that is already available to discuss the real pressing problems of the nation.

What's worse, most of the mainstream media are not only selective but biased as well. The television news operations of ABC, NBC, CBS, CNN and MSNBC are institutionally hostile toward conservative ideas and those who espouse them. So they don't just ignore the real problems. They actively seek to convince you that the real problems are the ones that would lead you to elect Democrats.

Many will argue that Fox News Channel and Fox Business Channel are just as biased in favor of the right. Let's get disclosure out of the way here: I am under contract as a contributor to both networks, so I just told you my bias. I recognize that these networks lean to the right but I am convinced that they are more serious about at least trying to present both sides of the story than the left-leaning outlets I mentioned above.

But having said that, you should make up your own mind and consider the limitations of every media outlet, as well as the manner in which they report and the news judgment they exercise in choosing what to focus on.

And don't think your local newspaper is any better. Sometimes they can give you better insight on a local story, but if you read national news in your local paper, they usually pull that from one of the leading wire services— the most widespread of which is the Associated Press. The AP used to be a straight just-the-facts source of information, but during the George W. Bush administration the AP adopted what it called "accountability journalism."[1] This may sound OK— who could object to holding people accountable?—

but in practice it became little more than a self-issued license to write opinionated propaganda under the guise of news reporting. Your local newspaper might add its own headline, but you're still reading thinly disguised propaganda.

Even worse is the "fact checking" genre exemplified by the likes of Politifact and FactCheck.org. These very biased outfits claim to judge the truth or fiction of what politicians say[2], but if you read their analysis carefully, you'll see that what they really do is pass judgment on information through the prism of their own left-wing bias.

This is not to say you should avoid the media entirely. I don't. But you should recognize that you simply can't depend on them to help you understand the real problems facing this nation. You need to be proactive in seeking out your own, more thoughtful sources.

If you really want to know what's going on and what it means, I suggest you watch, read and listen to a variety of sources— including those whose viewpoints disagree with yours. Some I would recommend include:

- *The Wall Street Journal* editorial page, followed closely by the *WSJ*'s news pages (most of the time).
- The Heritage Foundation's *The Daily Signal*.
- C-SPAN, which actually allows you to watch sessions of Congress live without the media's filter of "analysis."
- *National Review*, which has been the leader in conservative thought since the 1950s.

- *Forbes*, which delves into economic issues much more deeply than you typically see in the MSM.
- RedState.com, which is run by my friend Erick Erickson, who sometimes substitutes as host of my radio show.
- HotAir.com, an excellent conservative news and commentary site anchored by the highly respected Ed Morrissey, Mary Katharine Ham and anonymous blogger Allahpundit.
- Western Journalism.com

Of course, HermanCain.com! We give you timely news and commentary throughout each day. Also, the Herman Cain Radio Show, which you can listen to 24/7. That's right! Just go to Cain247.com anytime, anywhere on any digital device with internet access. And, CainRadioRaw.com, which has no interruptions, no commercials, and is just pure radio commentary!

I would also recommend some sources on the left, not because I agree with them but because I think they report well and do a good job of challenging all points of view in a useful way, including:

- *The Washington Post*, which is thorough in its reporting and often intellectually honest about the shortcomings of their own side.

Bloomberg, which has some depth to its economic and financial reporting even if their bias is a bit to the left for my tastes.

I would also suggest you take the initiative to receive information in other ways, such as:

- Get on the e-mail list for your congressman and your senators. That doesn't mean you should accept without question everything they tell you, but this would give you access to information they put out that the media chooses—for whatever reason—not to cover.

Set your Google News settings to topics of great importance. I'll let you know in this book what I think those topics should be, but you will ultimately decide for yourself.

As for social media, understand that it is both a resource and a trap. It's a place where you can learn about developments instantly and interact with other people who can add context and understanding. If you follow the right sources, you can not only learn what they know but you also can interact directly with them about it. But social media is also a place where you can be told all kinds of things that are not true. Remember "hands up, don't shoot?" Just about everyone believed that was a real part of the Ferguson, Missouri/Michael Brown story because it was circulated so widely on social media. But it wasn't true, as the subsequent investigation showed. Even so, to this day many people think it was true because they heard it on social media.

If you rely on social media for information, be discerning when it comes to who posts information and where it came from. Even information you want to believe, because it confirms your own biases, might be from a source of sensationalism rather than dependable, confirmed information.

The reason I decided to devote the first chapter of this book to the public being informed is that most politicians will not solve problems unless the public demands it. Even if they know the problems are serious, they are reluctant to take action for fear the public won't like the solutions and will punish them. I'm not saying this is good leadership— in fact, it's terrible leadership— but it is the nature of our political culture. While we try to elect better leaders, we should also get the public pressing the ones we have now to work on the right problems. If you stay better informed and can identify the right problems, then you can become part of the process by which we get to the right solutions.

It's really not that difficult to keep yourself well informed, especially given the nature of information technology today. What's important, though, is that you understand the sources that are substantive and trustworthy, and that you keep an eye on them most closely.

As for my assertion that the mainstream media are not that good a source for understanding the real problems facing this nation, that deserves a chapter all its own. So let's get to it.

# CHAPTER 2

## BIAS AND TRIVIA

Why people don't learn about the right
problems from the media

If there's been one discussion of media bias, there have
been a million. Pointing it out is like pointing out that the
sun is hot or that water is wet.

But if we really want to understand why our nation is
so fixated on the wrong solutions to the wrong problems,
we need to recognize that media bias is about more than
ideology. Yes, the political leanings of the mainstream
media are overwhelmingly liberal. We've all seen the
surveys that show legacy reporters vote Democrat more
than 80 percent of the time. Many of us have cited the

excellent work of the Media Research Center that documents the positive/negative tilt of media coverage, and how it consistently favors Democrats.

But liberal media bias is only the beginning of the problem. The media are also biased in favor of trivia. Sometimes it's trivia related to politics, like poll results or someone's "gaffe" on the stump. Sometimes it's pure trivia like Miley Cyrus twerking or Kylie Jenner's lip fillers (whatever those are). But even in what passes for the substantive discussion of policy, the media obsess over low-impact stories.

Over the past year, some of the stories they've covered extensively include:

- Gay marriage
- The minimum wage
- Alleged police brutality
- Hillary Clinton's visit to Chipotle in her Scooby van
- What various politicians say about evolution
- Gun control
- Who said what about Megyn Kelly
- Whether it's OK to use the term "anchor babies"
- Global warming
- Hate speech graffiti
- Income inequality

And of course, various polls and stories about which candidate has raised how much money

Now I am not saying that none of the above topics deserve any attention at all, although I would certainly argue that some of them deserve none whatsoever. But can anyone who understands what drives this nation's economy seriously suggest they deserve more coverage than the following?

- The details of the latest horrendous report on GDP growth
- All the capital that is sitting overseas because U.S. companies would pay a massive tax if they brought it home
- The record departure of workers from America's labor force
- The huge fiscal problems of ObamaCare exchanges, along with the narrowing of physician networks and exploding use of emergency rooms for routine care
- The money Americans spend every year paying professionals to help them comply with the tax code
- The constant, politically motivated manipulation of our currency.
- The effect of government restrictions on the production and distribution of domestic energy sources

- The growing influence of unions and the problems they present for job creation, especially as the Obama administration tips the scales in their favor
- The fact that Democrats did not pass a budget for five years
- The soaring national debt, which stands at more than $18 trillion as I write this

The coming crisis of unfunded entitlement mandates, which some estimate at more than $100 trillion[1]

The topics I listed here get occasional coverage, but they don't get anywhere near as much as the topics listed in the first group. Yet no serious person could argue that the first group of topics is as important or influential to the nation's health and prosperity as the second group.

So why do the media obsess over the former and very lightly cover the latter?

You could argue that the second group of stories doesn't lend itself to ongoing coverage, because there are not new developments on a daily basis. But I'd argue the same is true of the first group. There are not daily developments on gay marriage or global warming or income inequality. Mostly there are just reports of things people say about them, and sometimes hyped-up scandals because someone said something that was thought to be controversial.

Remember all the coverage of the pizza place in Indiana that said— in response to a media question— that they would not cater a gay wedding? That was not a substantive development of any kind. It was a lot of hyperventilating about an opinion someone expressed. There was no reason that reporter needed to ask the question in the first place, let alone cover the answer to the extent that they did. Granted, the coverage provided some useful revelations about the fascist tendencies of the American left, but that doesn't mean the story was really newsworthy in the first place.

If the media were interested, they could cover the stories I listed in the second group just as doggedly. They could track down people who have left the workforce and find out why they did so, then go to economic experts for their reactions, and to policymakers to find out their preferred policy solutions.

They could talk to the CEOs of companies that operate overseas and would like to bring their capital back to the U.S., but would face a huge cost in the form of the repatriated profits tax if they did. They could ask these CEOs how it would impact the company's ability to create jobs, and to produce quality products at a competitive price, if they lost that much capital paying this tax. They could then go to the liberals who insist on keeping this tax in place and find out why they insist on doing so. They could look at the budgetary implications of repealing it. That would be good, comprehensive coverage.

They could also dive headlong into the details of the federal budget, especially now that, with Republicans once again in charge on Capitol Hill, we actually have one again. Instead of focusing on the political machinations of the budget, they could tell us what's really in it. What are we spending on entitlement programs? What are we spending on ObamaCare subsidies? What are we spending on defense and how is it being allocated? What are we spending on things like aid to states and cities, and would we be better off just letting them keep the money in the first place?

Most Americans don't know the details of any of this, and that's one of the reasons the political class can get away with ignoring the real problems we face. And I lay this solely at the feet of the media because of the stories they choose to cover.

People know about the auto repair shop owner in Grandville, Michigan who doesn't want to serve gay customers, but they don't know the fiscal health of Social Security.

They know that some college had a campus-wide "teach in" because of something spray-painted on a wall, but they don't know what they owe as their share of the national debt.

They know that people are protesting for a $15-an-hour minimum wage, but they don't know that in cities where it happened, many of the same people lost their jobs because they priced themselves right out of the labor market.

They know that Hillary Clinton went to Chipotle, but they don't know she wants to "topple the 1 percent" (and they probably don't know she's part of the 1 percent).[2]

They know there was a lot of political tussling over the budget, but they don't how much we spend, or on what, or why, or what it represents as a percentage of our GDP, or how it affects the creation of wealth, or why that should even matter to them.

And none of this is because the American people are stupid. If these stories were reported in substantive detail, they would absolutely read, watch and listen to them. They would be able to recognize the relevance of these matters to their real lives. But it's easy for them to find stories like the ones in the first group above. It's a chore—doable, to be sure, but still a chore—to find stories like the ones in the second group.

I realize you could make the argument that people who really want to know what's important could make the effort to find those stories. You can argue that it's not that difficult to do with the availability of online news searches these days. And you can also argue—and many of you will—that the "less important" stories about trivia get a lot more web traffic, thus seeming to confirm the news judgment of the media who cover the trivia at the expense of the substance.

But I would say a couple of things in response to that. First, poor news judgment is still poor news judgment no matter what readers do. Reporters and editors claim we can trust them to make good decisions about the information we really need to know. If they make ridiculous decisions instead, and justify it by pointing to the click counters, then they've put the lie to their claims that they possess good news judgment.

But beyond that, it's only natural to expect that people will be more familiar with stories that get covered more.

Political junkies and people who work in and around the media might have all the time in the world to sit around and do Google news searches. Ordinary people are working 8-to-5, taking their kids to ballgames, having dinner with the family, and going to the movies. The political class thinks this makes them shallow and self-centered. I disagree. I think people who sit around obsessing over omnibus budgets and political polls when they could be having an ice cream cone with their kids are the weird ones.

So if normal people only have time to skim the top headlines because they're busy living their lives, then I think it's reasonable to ask the media to make those top headlines about the things that really matter. Too often, they don't, which is why we end up with so much focus on the trivial and too little focus on the issues that really matter.

Now, does liberal bias play a part in the media's obsession over the trivial? Of course it does. I think that works mainly in three ways:

First, the mainstream media consist of liberal elitists who look down their noses at the average American. There are exceptions, of course, but liberal elitism is the prevailing culture of the media, so story decisions are made in the context of that culture. Because they take such a dim view of the people who consume their product, they start with the presumption that people are not interested in the substantive depth of stories. They put more resources into covering the Kardashians or the royal baby than they put into covering the ins and outs of the federal tax code because they are convinced you are "fascinated" by the former and don't care about the latter. In other words, they think you are a shallow fool who wouldn't be interested in serious news if they gave it to you.

Second, their notion of substance is colored by their ideology. They really don't think it's a big story that the federal government spends more than 21 percent of GDP, so they don't treat it as one. They don't see why the tax code should be replaced because a complicated system that punishes wealth and productivity sounds about right to them. So why report on the problems it causes? What problems? They don't think the breakdown of the family is much of an issue because they don't have very high regard for the institution of the family anyway.

So their stories about income inequality and global warming reflect a genuine, if totally misguided, belief that these issues really matter on a broad scale. What's more, they've been trained to see stories like the ones I listed in the second group above as "Republican talking points," and one of the first things they learned as journalists is that it's not their job to report that. That's why you see these issues covered in media clearly labeled as conservative, but in media that pretend to be unbiased (but of course are really liberal), they are ignored. The mainstream media have written off entire topic areas as mere right-wing propaganda, and they actually think they're being objective by ignoring them.

The third point, of course, is that the media absolutely have an agenda to help Democrats and to hurt Republicans.

Let's not pretend otherwise. They often scoff at this assertion by mocking the notion that they sit around and conspire about how to screw the GOP in their coverage. And it's true that for the most part they don't do that. But they don't need to. Their culture drives their agenda.

Consider the experience of Sharyl Attkisson, the rare conservative who rose to a prominent mainstream media position with CBS. Attkisson regularly had her stories about the IRS scandal and about Benghazi spiked by her bosses, who didn't like that they made the Obama administration look bad. Attkisson could do little about it because she operated in a culture that was hostile to aggressive reporting about the Obama administration. The prevailing attitude in the newsroom was that anyone pursuing such stories too doggedly was doing the work of the Republicans, and it was easy to justify killing these stories on that basis. I've interviewed Sharyl on my radio show and I am happy to know she is still thriving as an investigative journalist, despite what her bosses did to stop her progress.

If media bias presents an obvious problem in that it helps to elect Democrats, it presents a more subtle problem in that it discourages Republican candidates for office—let alone Republican officeholders—from talking about the kinds of problems that really impact the nation.

Republican candidates listen to their consultants very carefully, and their consultants tell them that if they hope to win the election, they have to win the news cycles. How do you do that? You do that by staging media events or other initiatives designed to curry favorable coverage. It's very difficult to do that by celebrating the virtues of business entrepreneurs because the media think they are greedy robber barons. It's just as hard to do it by talking about replacing the tax code, or about currency manipulation, or about opening up new opportunities for oil companies.

Your consultants will tell you those are losers. They'll tell you to go to a school and read to the children, or to have a "town hall meeting" with seniors. They'll tell you the optics of such things are better, and they will make you look more like a down-to-earth, normal person—and that is the sort of thing that will get you favorable media coverage.

So a Republican candidate might favor replacing the tax code or going back to the gold standard, and if you delve deeply into his or her website you may find those positions spelled out. But if you just read typical media coverage of the campaign, you won't hear about those things.

Why does that matter? It matters because governing effectively requires the consent of the governed. How many Republicans have you seen elected to Congress who supposedly favored certain things, but once they were in office they made no progress toward accomplishing them?

A lot of that has to do with the fact that voters did not elect them mainly on the basis of those issue positions. And that is because they were de-emphasized by campaign consultants in order to secure the most positive coverage possible from the liberal media.

So we don't work on the right problems because even the candidates who believe in working on the right problems don't think they're political winners—at least to the extent they think they need positive media coverage to win.

That's a huge impact of liberal media bias on the priorities we choose for our nation. The people aren't demanding that we focus on these issues because they don't realize how important they are. And that's because the mainstream media don't tell them about these issues, and pandering politicians don't emphasize them in their campaign themes because they don't think it's what the people want to hear.

One reason the mainstream media are liberal is the simple experience of being a reporter. People are more likely to be conservative when they've risked capital to build something, or learned about the business world from the inside. Most reporters have never done that. They may have interviewed business leaders but they've never experienced what it's like to be one or to work for one. They've spent their entire careers making a pretty modest wage, which maybe gets a little better with time if their union gets them a little raise.

Those who get tired of working for the paltry wages of journalism and want to do better tend to leave and go into a different field where they can utilize their communication skills to make more money. Those who are left in the newsroom often consider these folks sell-outs. They think the true virtue of a journalist is to spend your whole life working on a news staff for paltry wages and feeling morally superior about it. I feel this way having been interviewed many times over the years, by reporters of various experience levels.

There's another reason reporters tend to favor government as the solution to every problem, and it has to do with the way their career paths work. When a young reporter gets hired by the local newspaper or television station, there's a pecking order of the most desirable and glamorous beats. And at the top of the food chain is always the governmental beats—the city hall reporter, the Capitol reporter. These are seen as the plumb assignments. The reporter who starts out on the business beat, in addition to not knowing very much about business (which presents problems all its own), is trying to earn his or her way out of that beat and onto the beats covering government.

This has the effect of orienting the media toward government as the center of all action, and as the source of all solutions to society's problems. They sit down with elected officials and ask questions that start with, "What are you going do about…?" They don't want to hear the elected official say, "Nothing. People need to solve that problem for themselves." On the glamorous governmental beat, these reporters want to report that the people they cover are trying to change the world. If government is humble, limited and minimalist, that beat they spent years working to get assigned is suddenly a lot less glamorous. Reporters are liberal in part because they are very focused on government and politics, and it seems natural to them that this is where the action should be.

So the experience of being a reporter tends to weed out the conservatives and leave the liberals as the lifers. That's got a lot to do with why the prevailing point of view in news coverage is almost always left of center. Because the people who make journalism their life's work—never having experienced what it's like to be an entrepreneur or a top corporate executive—are overwhelmingly liberal.

What can we do about that? We don't want to take away the liberal media's freedom of speech, but we can and should take away their market share. Fox News has certainly done it in cable news, regularly pulling ratings that exceed those of the liberal networks CNN and MSNBC combined. With the advent of internet streaming and smart TVs, the barriers to entry into the news market are lower than ever. There is no reason we should not see more successful challenges to the liberal media.

I would argue, though, that some of the conservative attempts to do this so far have fallen short because they didn't do a good enough job of reporting and delivering information. You have to be more than a right-wing propaganda outfit if you want to influence the public. You have to first serve the public by giving them the information they need. Conservative-leaning news organizations who understand how to do this will be successful. Those who just want to make political points will not.

If we continue to rely on the existing mainstream media, the public will never truly understand the right problems we should be working on, let alone the right solutions. They'll continue to think global warming and campus sexism are the most important things happening in America—while our debt balloons out of control and our tax code chokes off job-creating businesses.

I would encourage anyone reading this book to actively seek out other sources of information beyond the liberal media. Read economic news sites like Forbes and Fortune. Read conservative news sites like Red State, TownHall, HotAir, Breitbart and, of course, HermanCain.com! And maybe someone out there will decide to start the media competition that will help redefine the terms of public discourse in this country.

We need to talk about the right solutions, and if the mainstream media are leading the discussion, then that will never happen. So let's take their role as leaders of the discussion away from them.

# CHAPTER 3

## NO ONE SAID IT WOULD BE EASY

The Five Hardest Problems
America Must Solve

The right problems America needs to be working on are easy to see if people open their eyes and their minds. This chapter and the next will open your eyes and make you think beyond the media's lens. Politicians work to keep people in the dark, and most of the media works to keep people narrow-minded about the most important issues of our time.

Specifically, I'm going to give you nine of them.

Now if some of your favorite issues are not on the list, that doesn't mean I don't think they matter. Remember, this is a book about leverage. It's about identifying the high-impact issues that, once solved, should lead to improvements on a lot of other fronts, too.

For example, is the state of the labor force an important issue? Absolutely. We talk about it all the time on my radio show and on my website. So why isn't it on the list? It's not on the list because trying to fix the labor force in isolation is neither very strategic nor is it something the federal government is in a good position to do.

By contrast, replacing the tax code is on the list because the tax code is an essential function of the federal government, so not only is it something Washington can do, but it will have a positive impact on the labor force as well.

Another issue very important to me is faith. I think it's crucial that this nation put God back at the center of everything we do. So why isn't that on the list? Because that isn't something the federal government does, per se. The federal government needs to stop being hostile toward people and institutions of faith, and respecting our Constitution (which is on the list) would eliminate those policies of hostility. Let that happen and people of faith can do their work. I don't want the government—not even the president—trying to be the leader of that effort because neither our society nor the church was ever designed for things to work that way.

So those are two examples of issues that are very important, but they're not the right problems for political leaders to focus on because a) political leaders are neither well-positioned nor particularly capable of addressing them directly; and b) they are not the major leverage issues that will cause other situations to improve as a result.

With that said, let's start to go through the nine problems our leaders must regard as the highest priorities to solve. We'll look at what the issue is, why it's one of the right problems, and how it might be solved, as well as why politicians may not want to solve it.

We'll look at five problems in this chapter and four more in the next. The issues we address in this chapter are more difficult than those in the next, because years of foolish policies have created such serious problems that it will take a lot of effective problem-solving to deal with them. I wouldn't say the problems we address in the next chapter are "easy," but all they really need to be solved are the correct public policy changes.

So let's start with the five most difficult ones:

### *Balance the Budget*

Note, I did not say "reduce the deficit." I said balance the budget. It is a problem when you spend more than you take in. When you do it every single year as a matter of course, with no plan to stop doing so, it's way beyond a problem. It's systematic fiscal suicide.

I'm sure you've heard the arguments that a family who habitually spends beyond its means will end up in bankruptcy or worse. I'm sure you know that many states have balanced budget amendments to their state constitutions, and are required every year to make sure they don't spend more than they take in from revenue.

I'm sure you've also heard the retorts from the political class. It's not the same thing, they say. Most U.S. debt is held by the public so we really just owe it to ourselves, they assure us. We can't balance the budget now because we need to make investments! Oh, and if you really want to balance the budget, why won't you "ask the rich to pay their fair share"?

These debates go on interminably, and keep us from getting to the heart of the matter. Every year we add to the national debt, which now stands at more than $18 trillion. We do several things—all of them bad:

We add to the difficulty of balancing the budget in this and subsequent years because we have to pay the interest on that debt every single year. In 2015, the Congressional Budget Office estimates we'll pay $227 billion just in interest on the debt.[1] To get a sense of perspective, 30 years ago that would have paid for the entire defense budget. Now we spend it just for the privilege of being able to borrow money. In other words, we're flushing it down the toilet every year. We're paying it out and getting nothing for it.

Nothing.

And it gets worse. I do not subscribe to the view of the political class that the CBO is infallible, but let's use their numbers here just for the sake of perspective. The CBO also estimates that interest on the debt will increase to $480 billion by 2019, and to $722 billion by 2024.[2]

Understand, this does not retire a penny of principle. It pays interest only. Maybe you've taken out a loan at some point in your life, and for the first year of the loan the bank allowed you to pay interest only on the loan. You might have thought you were getting a break because your payments weren't very high. No, you weren't. Those interest payments to the bank were a boon to the bank and a raw deal for you. They got to collect the interest without reducing the principle you owed them at all. Once your interest-only period ran out, you still owed every penny you borrowed, and your payments suddenly skyrocketed.

Everyone who has a home mortgage knows that in the early years of the mortgage, you pay mostly interest, and only in the later years are you retiring principle at any sort of respectable rate. That's why you might pay more than $300,000 on a mortgage for a home you bought at $150,000.

But at least in the examples I described above, you eventually start paying down the principle. That is not the case with the national debt. We never pay any principle. Even short-term bonds, which we have to pay off in a given amount of time, we merely refinance. So the national debt may be only $18 trillion, but paying it off is going to see us spend a lot more than $18 trillion because we spend so much every year just in interest.

And every year we run a deficit, even the relatively "small" deficits like the $468 billion we're running in 2015, we add to the debt, add to the future principle we'll have to pay off, and add to those interest payments that are going to balloon within a decade.[3]

Here is another problem with the debt. One of the things keeping the interest payments from ballooning out of control today is the fact that the Federal Reserve Board is holding interest rates at ridiculously low levels. They are doing that largely for political reasons. They say it's to reduce the cost of borrowing in the hope that companies will finance expansions and more job creation (rather than hiring as a result of real sustainable profits, which is what businesses should do), but it's also to mask the cost of the national debt.[4] If the Fed raised interest rates to what they probably should be, you'd see interest on the debt explode immediately to the levels discussed above.

Now maybe you're one of those people who was once in debt and worked hard to pay it all off. Way to go! You, of all people, understand well how frustrating it was to work hard and earn a lot of money, only to turn around and pay it all out to creditors. You were working like crazy and earning good money, but probably not living like it because you didn't get to keep the money. You understand it was your own fault because you let yourself get into debt, but it still stung, and if it took you a few years to pay off all those debts; there were surely times when you wondered if all that hard work you were doing was really all worth it.

Now apply the same principles to the United States of America. If we balanced the budget tomorrow, we'd owe more than $18 trillion. If we ran surpluses of $200 billion, we'd have to pay every penny of those surpluses for 90 years just to pay off the principle, not to mention the interest. As a nation, we'd have to produce an awful lot and exercise a heck of a lot of fiscal discipline for more than a generation just to get back to square one.[5]

And the scenario I just described is wildly optimistic. I think we could do it, but we won't even be able to give ourselves a chance to do it if we don't stop borrowing.

We need to balance the budget, and the sooner the better. I support Friends of the Article V Convention, which seeks 38 states to call a Constitutional Convention of the States to pass a Balanced Budget Amendment. The majority of states are required by their constitutions to balance their budgets, and there is no reason the federal government should not have to meet the same requirement.

Balancing the budget would allow us to a) stop adding to our debt burden; b) stop adding to the cost of paying interest on the debt; c) stop looking for new excuses to raise taxes on producers; d) start down the road of paying off our debts.

There are a lot of other reasons we need to balance the budget. One of which is that we owe $1.3 trillion to China. China is not our friend in a geopolitical sense at all. Their strategic interests are very much in opposition to ours, and we need to be strong and aggressive in the defense of our interests.

But you know what? It's very difficult to defend your interests vis-à-vis a party to which you owe $1.3 trillion. It's a hammer they can hold over your head whenever they think they need to, and there's nothing you can do about it. Owing another country money puts us in a compromised position—and that directly affects our ability to make decisions concerning our national security.

The simple fact is that anyone is better off—individual, company or nation—when you're financially independent. That party to whom you owe money… they own you. And America's leaders have been systematically putting us and keeping us in that position for generations because they refuse to limit their spending to what they take in.

For all these reasons, balancing the budget is one of the right problems. Solve it, and we can tax people less, better prioritize what we do spend, and make better decisions about our national interests. A balanced budget would free up far more capital for investment in productivity, jobs and wealth creation. It's a high-leverage priority and our leaders need to tackle it. Now.

As for how to do it, there are plenty of steps they could take if only Congress had the political will.

Let's start by acknowledging that the biggest part of the federal budget is federal entitlements—a category that has long included Social Security, Medicare and Medicaid, and now also includes ObamaCare. Restructuring the first three and eliminating the fourth are among the priorities we discuss in this book, so we'll save the details of that when we get to it. Suffice it to say, reducing what we spend on these programs is essential to balancing the budget.

Next we need to look at entire federal departments and agencies that either don't need to exist at all, or could see their roles seriously curtailed. The Department of Education could either be eliminated entirely or could be scaled back to a bare-bones office that helps to coordinate some of what is happening in the states. No one should be looking to the federal government to exercise leadership on something like educating kids, which happens at the local and state level.

The Environmental Protection Agency is destroying industries and encroaching on people's property rights. The entire idea of the EPA should be reconstituted, and we should end up with a much smaller EPA that has much less power, or perhaps no EPA at all.

The Department of Health and Human Services is able to abuse its power far more extensively now that ObamaCare is law. But even before ObamaCare, HHS duplicated much of what's already being done in the states. There is no reason Washington needs to be in the health and human services business at all.

As for the Internal Revenue Service, it would have much less to do if we could replace the tax code (another priority of this book). But even with the existing tax code, the IRS spends far too much time and money using its power to serve the interests of its political masters rather than doing what it's supposed to do, which is collect revenue. An IRS that truly functioned as a "service" would be trying to help taxpayers, not abuse them, while operating in a politically neutral fashion with the only goal of bringing in the money the government needs to operate.

Three years after we learned of the IRS abusing its authority to harass conservative political organizations, it should be clear to anyone that the agency has far exceeded its supposed mission and needs to be restrained.

I don't mean to suggest that these are the only departments or agencies that could be targeted for elimination. I question whether we need a Federal Department of Energy, for example, and even departments that have ostensibly important functions like Homeland Security and Veterans' Affairs don't necessarily need to be as big as they are to do their jobs. Don't even get me started about all the waste in the Department of Transportation. Food stamps are completely out of control, and the Department of Agriculture oversees that program. They actually advertise for new food stamp recipients!

At the very least, they could restrict the use of food stamps to items poor people truly need—and don't believe their insistence that this is too hard to do. All you need to do is program the EBT cards so that they can only be used for certain approved Universal Product Codes. It would be easy to do. Politicians (especially Democrats) don't really want to do it because they like having people dependent on government for as many things as possible.

Now let's talk for a second about earmarks. Sen. Jeff Flake of Arizona is getting a lot of attention and credit lately for being a champion of pork-cutting. This is a hard thing to get rid of because just about every member of Congress loves being able to claim he or she brought home the bacon to the district. Earmarks are spending items set aside for very specific projects, and they come from a pot of money that's set aside for projects of this nature. Members of Congress—even the ones who claim to be against earmarks—put in requests for projects in their districts, and if those projects get funded then they put out press releases making sure everyone knows they brought the money home from Washington.

Politicians do not want to give up the ability to do that sort of thing, which is why earmarks continue. But when the people start to demand that earmarks stop—because they are really just a way for politicians to buy your vote with your money—then it will stop because politicians will be paying a price for their spending instead of reaping a reward. It might also stop if a new president exercised real leadership on the issue, and that is also a matter we will deal with in a subsequent chapter.

Let me highlight one other item, as it's an example of the sort of thing that drives up federal spending but is largely hidden from the public. I lived in Omaha for 14 years, and one time after we moved, I went back to visit. I was very surprised to see how lavishly the Omaha airport had been renovated—especially an elaborate sculpture at the entrance to the airport. It was very nice, but I was having a hard time understanding why it needed to be there, so I asked someone at the airport about it.

He told me it's a federal law that airports have to spend a certain percentage of what they get from the federal government on artwork. Seriously. It's hard to figure why Congress would pass such a law, but this sort of thing is more common than you think. Some artsy type lobbies to get a member of a key committee to add this to a bill, and it ends up in the final language—maybe because that congressman gave the other committee members some things they wanted in return—and the bill passes on a floor vote and is signed into law. Most people don't even realize it's there, but there it is.

So federal money is being spent on sculptures and all kinds of other things that are nice but not really needed, because someone got language into a bill calling for it, and the law is the law. Rooting out things like this might not save trillions, but it might save billions, and it would surely go a long way toward exposing the sort of chicanery that gives us this type of spending in the first place.

Do you know that if the federal government reverted to its size and scope of the year 2007, we would be running a sizeable surplus today?[6] Do you seriously mean to tell me we didn't have enough government in 2007?

The idea that we could balance the budget quickly is seen as radical by the political class, because they never want to scale back anything government does. But in practical terms, all it would require is some rational decisions and the setting of some priorities. It is eminently doable. People in Washington don't want to do it (more on that shortly), but they absolutely could.

### Replace the Tax Code

There's a reason I briefly sat atop the polls in the 2012 primary race, and it wasn't because I said "Uzbeki-beki-beki-beki-stan-stan" or "shucky ducky." I said those things because, unlike the political reporters I said them to, I enjoy humor. But that's a topic for another day.

I believe the reason I shot to the top of the polls was my 9-9-9 tax plan. Now if you ask your average political pundit today, they'll either pretend not to remember 9-9-9 or they'll claim it was some sort of silly gimmick. At the time, though, the public understood exactly what 9-9-9 was. It was a proposal to throw out the entire federal tax code and replace it with a new, simple system that consisted solely of three taxes:

- A 9 percent income tax
- A 9 percent federal sales tax
- A 9 percent business tax

There was more detail to it, of course, and we explained all that in my last book, 9-9-9: An Army of Davids. But the details were applied to make a very simple tax code work in a very simple way for taxpayers. No longer would they spend billions trying to comply with a complicated tax code, trying to shelter income, trying to manipulate their decisions to minimize their tax liability. And no longer would people be subjected to IRS audits based on deductions and exemptions they claimed, because the system wouldn't have many deductions or exemptions. People wouldn't need any. The low rates and simply applied formulas would render them unnecessary.

9-9-9 resonated with ordinary people who are tired of a tax code designed to serve politicians and not the country as a whole. I am not saying it's the only way you could replace the tax code, although I believed then, and still believe today, it would be an excellent one.

You could also do it with a simple flat tax—again applying the same very low rate across the board and eliminating most, if not all, deductions. You could also do it with the national consumption tax known as the FairTax—which would rely entirely on taxes on retail sales. Some have said the FairTax would eliminate the IRS altogether. I'm not sure that's true because someone would need to collect the revenue from the retailers, but it would eliminate the IRS as a factor in the lives of ordinary Americans.

The tax code is one of the right problems to work on because the tax code is absolutely toxic to American growth and prosperity. It is so complicated and difficult to comply with, it has spawned an entire industry of consultants who do nothing but help people figure it all out. Now I'm sure a lot of accountants and tax consultants wouldn't be too happy with a simplified tax code that renders them unnecessary, but let me ask you a question: If the federal government went and dumped two feet of snow on every road in America, then we all had to pay billions of dollars to hire snow plow drivers to clear the roads, would that sound like a good way to create jobs? Of course not, even most liberals wouldn't think that was a good idea (unless the plow drivers were unionized). But that's exactly what we do with the tax code. It's the snow on the road. All the tax accountants are the plow drivers, and we have to hire them every year to clear the road just so we can pay our taxes without getting in trouble with the IRS.

And it's not just the money we have to spend. It's also the way businesses and individuals make decisions. Because the tax code contains so many incentives and enticements—things that give you a break on your taxes if you do things politicians want you to do—businesses and individuals make far too many decisions based on the tax benefits rather than on what would bring them to growth and prosperity.

What would happen if you simply paid a flat percentage of everything you made—and no matter how much that was, you'd still pay the same percentage? What if it was just that simple? You wouldn't have to spend a lot of time developing "tax strategies" because there would be no need to be strategic. You'd just have to make sure you paid the requisite percentage and be done with it.

Liberals and the media argue that such a system would be regressive on the poor. That is easily proven false. A regressive tax means the poor pay a higher percentage than the rich. No one is proposing that. Many have even proposed that everyone should receive a sizeable personal exemption, so you wouldn't pay any tax on the first, say, $10,000 of your earnings—with the flat rate kicking in only at dollar number 10,001. That would actually keep the tax quite progressive, since the percentage you'd pay in tax of what you actually make would be much lower if you don't earn that much beyond the personal exemption.

Of course, liberals and the media will carp about any tax code that isn't designed to punish the rich simply for being rich, and to redistribute America's wealth.

Others will argue that you could never get rid of all the deductions and exemptions because they are too deeply embedded in the tax code. And yes, I know they are, which is why the first thing that needs to happen is for Congress to pass, and the president to sign, a bill that repeals the entire federal tax code. That's right. Repeal the entire thing. Done. Gone. This would, in one fell swoop, eliminate all those special favors and considerations in the code.

Then, and only then, do you pass a second law establishing the new, simplified tax code.

Back in the 1990s, I had the honor of serving on the Kemp Commission that looked into revising the tax code. The principles embraced by that commission were that the code had to be simpler, fairer, flatter and more visible. Any of the three major proposals for replacing the tax code—the Flat Tax, the FairTax and 9-9-9—achieve those objectives.

But this cannot be achieved by tweaking or trying to "reform" the existing tax code. And it certainly won't be achieved by proposing ever more tax credits, which has been the favored approach among Republicans in recent years. All tax credits do is create one more situation in which people feel compelled to do what politicians want them to do in order to get a little break on their taxes.

The right kind of tax code would be one in which it doesn't matter what you do or how you do it, so long as you pay the required (and very low) percentage assessed on what you've earned. If you want to buy equipment, do it because you need it to make more stuff and that can help you make more money. Don't do it as a tax strategy. If you want to offer your employees health benefits, do it as a retention strategy. Don't do it to save on your taxes. If you want to give your grandchild a condo, do it because you're a nice grandparent. Don't do it to minimize the tax burden on your future estate.

We make far too many decisions in this country because of taxes, and it's one of the reasons we need to get rid of the tax code.

When I was working on the 9-9-9 plan, economist Stephen Moore said it would be "rocket fuel for the economy." Our hope is that it would spur such robust economic activity that we could regularly see GDP growth of at least 4 to 5 percent on an annualized basis. And if we did that, by the way, the larger and healthier tax base would get us a long way toward solving that first problem of balancing the budget. It would also free up businesses to direct their capital in much more productive ways, thus allowing them to prosper more and create more jobs.

These are the reasons the tax code is one of the right problems to work on, and why getting rid of it entirely and starting over is the right solution.

### *Restructure Social Security*

Any time someone talks about changing Social Security, liberals shriek that they want to rob old people of what they've got coming after years of paying into the system.

News flash: I'm 70 years old as of December 13, 2015. I've been paying into the system since I was 17. I want to get what's coming to me too! And one thing I know is that this will not happen if we leave Social Security exactly as it is today. Because I realize this, my feeling is that I would be happy getting some of my money back, if it's part of a serious restructuring and not just more political tweaking.

Here's something you might not know. When Social Security was created during the Roosevelt administration, there were more than 40 younger people paying into the system for every older person drawing from it. Today, there are only three people paying into the system for every one person collecting.[7]

Life expectancy is much higher than it was 80 years ago, so there are more older people living longer.[8] There are also more younger people collecting Social Security for various reasons.[9] Oh, and in case you didn't know, there is no "Social Security Trust Fund."[10] That is fiction propped up by politicians. There is theoretically an account balance that belongs to Social Security, but in reality Congress raids Social Security money every year to paper over the real size of the federal budget deficit.[11] So if you go looking for the bank account wherein sits all the money that's been placed in safe keeping for America's present and future seniors, you will come up empty. That money's not there. What you paid into the system is not sitting somewhere waiting for you to collect it. It's been spent. And when the federal government pays Social Security benefits, it pays them out of current revenues (or it borrows the money) just like it funds everything else.[12]

Depending on who you ask, Social Security is expected to go under water anywhere from the next five years to the next 20. Right now, the federal government raids what's left of the FICA tax collections to pay for things that should come out of the general fund.[13] According to The Heritage Foundation, "In 2012, Social Security spent $55 billion more in benefits than it took in from its payroll tax and income tax."[14]

Even now, this is not going in a good direction. The program's own trustees estimate that Social Security will see a cash flow deficit of $77 billion by 2018.[15] After that, they project that the deficit will increase steeply because incomes available to pay for all the recipients will fall. This is a mess today, and it's about to become a much bigger one.

Meanwhile, forcing everyone to pay into—and rely on—Social Security is robbing a lot of people of the opportunity to do better in their retirement savings. That money that came out of your paycheck via the FICA tax could have been invested in a private fund that could have performed much better than Social Security. But you never had the chance to invest that money because the federal government mandated you hand it over to them so they could make you a promise not backed by any actual cash on hand.

One reason Social Security is one of the right problems is that it's an enormous piece of a federal budget we simply must reduce. And when liberals protest that Social Security isn't the problem because it pays for itself at the moment, that's sort of true but it misses the point. Yes, we pay for the spending (for now), but we're still spending it, and it's a function of the federal government that could be made much smaller and more affordable. Another reason is that many people would choose to go a different route in saving for their retirement if they had the choice, and they would have more secure retirements if they were allowed to make that choice.

And it would be better for them, and for the country, if they could.

So how do we do it? The best model I've seen comes from Chile, which radically transformed its version of Social Security—and badly needed to. Consider that today, the average FICA contribution is 12.5 percent. In Chile, they were having to take 27 percent just to break even. So they decided to give people the option of transitioning to a private account. More than 90 percent of the population chose that option, inspired I'm sure by the fact that once they owned the account, the money would belong to them and no one else, and they could decide the amount of the contribution they'd be making.[16]

A few years ago, Congressman Paul Ryan (R-Wisconsin) proposed something similar. Under his plan, Social Security would not have changed at all for anyone 55 or older—including a freeze on the system's obligations to those in that age group so they can reasonably plan for what they're going to get, but they also know it won't go up.

Those under 55 can also choose to stay in the system, but their benefits are likewise locked in. Or they can divert some or all of their savings to private accounts, which they control completely.[17] We're not talking about a government IOU. We're talking about real cash in a real account that they own. The amount put in your account would depend on the government's accrued obligation to you. But once it's in your account, you take it from there. The government's obligation to you is fulfilled and it's up to you to manage it as you move toward retirement.

Why would a person take that deal? Simple. It would allow the person to manage their retirement fund toward a better return than they would have gotten with Social Security. For those who would feel daunted by the task of managing their own retirement, they would simply stay in the current system. However, according to the Cato Institute, when Chile converted their system 93 percent of recipients chose to manage their accounts.[18]

Contrary to what liberals insist, this would not "destroy" Social Security. It would save it, because benefit obligations would be frozen even as people are allowed to exercise the option of moving to a different system.

If we still had 40 people paying into the system for everyone drawing benefits, a change like this would be much harder to undertake because the massive defections would seriously reduce the revenue available to pay current benefits. But as the system stands today, it's very doable.

And we need to do it, because the looming obligation of Social Security is a major threat to the nation's fiscal health. We need to learn from what happened to General Motors, which agreed in a decades-ago deal with the United Auto Workers to pay health care benefits for retirees. It seemed like a nice thing to do at the time, but by the collapse of 2008, GM was responsible for the healthcare costs of more than 100,000 people who were no longer contributing anything to the company.[19] This was probably the single biggest factor leading to the company's bankruptcy.

That is the same kind of bomb that's awaiting the American taxpayer when it comes to Social Security. We need to get a handle on it, and we need to do it now. I know politicians consider Social Security to be the "third rail of American politics," something they can never touch for fear of a backlash from seniors who vote.

But if you're trying to identify the right problems to work on, this one is an obvious choice. An urgent one too.

### Restructure Medicare and Medicaid

This is one of the trickiest problems to tackle because the crux of the problem is that the cost of health care overall has blown up so much. The basic idea of the two programs is not terrible. We need some sort of health safety net for the poor, and it makes sense that the program should be administered by the states. That's how Medicaid works.

And we need some sort of source of health insurance for the elderly, which is what Medicare is. It makes sense that people pay premiums for Medicare coverage instead of just treating it as a massive welfare program.

But both programs are still wildly expensive, and our future obligations to people through these programs have been estimated as high as $100 trillion. Part of the problem is that these programs were designed at a time when life expectancy was nowhere near what it is today, so the actuarial projections failed to account for many years of paying health benefits that are now standard to the program.

Another problem is that health care didn't cost in the mid-1960s what it costs today, because we hadn't yet seen the effects of third-party payers and malpractice lawsuits.

And of course, federal spending for health care will only grow because of ObamaCare. One thing the White House doesn't talk about much is that a significant number of those who have "gained coverage" under ObamaCare have really just enrolled in their respective states' expanded Medicaid coverage.

Whatever the cause, the government anticipates that its spending on Medicare and Medicaid will handsomely outpace economic growth over the next several years. This is from a 2013 report from the Centers for Medicare and Medicaid Services:[20]

Medicare
- Due to a deceleration in growth driven by sequestration and lower utilization across services, Medicare spending growth is projected to have slowed to 3.3 percent in 2013, down from 4.8

percent growth in 2012, and to have totaled $591.2 billion.

- Projected Medicare spending growth of 4.2 percent in 2014 reflects both an expected increase in use and intensity of Medicare services, alongside slow increases in payment rates. For 2015, Medicare growth is projected to slow to 2.7 percent, mostly due to lower payments to Medicare Advantage plans.

For 2016 through 2023, projected Medicare spending growth is expected to rebound to 7.3 percent per year due to increased enrollment by the baby boomers, increased utilization of care, and higher payment rates driven by improved economic conditions, which increase growth in the cost of input goods and services used to treat Medicare patients. These drivers in growth will be partially offset by slow growth in payment updates due to provisions in the Affordable Care Act and sequestration.

Medicaid

- Medicaid spending is anticipated to have grown 6.7 percent and to have reached $449.5 billion in 2013, driven by higher payment rates to primary care physicians called for in the Affordable Care Act, as well as actions by states that increased provider reimbursement rates and expanded benefits.

- Total Medicaid spending is projected to grow 12.8 percent in 2014 due to increased enrollment of nearly 8 million beneficiaries. Primarily driving the increase in enrollment are states that chose to expand coverage to adults up to 138 percent of the federal poverty level.

As some states are expected to expand their Medicaid programs after 2014, an additional 8.5 million people are expected to enroll in the program by 2016. Medicaid spending is expected to grow by 6.7 percent in 2015, and 8.6 percent in 2016. For 2016 to 2023, Medicaid spending growth is projected to be 6.8 percent per year on average.

Those growth numbers are astonishing. This nation's economy has been growing at an annual rate barely above 2 percent, and we're looking at healthcare costs expanding as much as four times that amount.

As it stands today, we're spending more than $582 billion a year on Medicare and more than $350 billion a year on Medicaid. That's more than a quarter of the entire federal budget, being taken up by these two programs. And they're expected to increase by as much as 8 percent annually for the next decade—at a time when we're not experiencing anywhere near the economic growth we would need to keep up with that kind of spending.

That doesn't even account for the hidden burden on the states who accepted the Medicaid expansion in ObamaCare—coming as it did with a limited-time commitment of federal dollars to cover the cost.

We simply have to reconceive the idea of these programs. There is no simple fix, but one place to start is the repeal of ObamaCare. Not only has ObamaCare added many more people to the Medicaid rolls, it has also imposed the economically insane rules that are causing people's premiums to go through the roof while narrowing their coverage options.

Regarding Medicare, I think it makes sense to look at the successful model Chile used to reform its version of Social Security and see if it can be applied to health care for the elderly too. I realize the two are not exactly the same— since you can set retirement benefits more easily than you can predict a person's healthcare costs. Nonetheless, the basic idea is that a person invests money in a fund that is used to pay for something they'll need, and Chile's system worked because it made the private sector pre-eminent both in investing the funds and in paying out the benefits.

I really don't want to empower the health insurance industry more than it already is, but it's better than saddling the taxpayers with costs like these. During the 2012 presidential campaign, vice presidential candidate Paul Ryan was outspoken in proposing that we move to a system in which the government provides support for seniors to pay their premiums to private insurers—and that leaves the paying of the benefits to those insurers. This was trashed by Democrats, of course, who insist that no promise can be trusted if it's not the government making it.

And that's absurd. The government is bankrupting itself by making these promises. It's the last party anyone should consider trustworthy given the nature of its obligations compared with the resources available to pay for them.

Any plausible idea for reconceiving Medicare and Medicaid should be on the table. And any real leader should be pushing it to the forefront—not hiding in the background out of fear of the political consequences. If the American people don't understand why this is absolutely necessary, then that's a failure of leadership of the political class. We need new leaders who can make the public understand. And quickly. This is an urgent problem and it has to be addressed now.

### *Secure the Border and Enforce Existing Immigration Laws*

Both parts of this equation are very difficult because of the fact that the issue has been neglected for so long. It's one thing to deport illegal aliens when there are a few thousand in the country, or even a few hundred thousand. It's quite another when there are more than 12 million, and they're here precisely because they know the government isn't interested in enforcing its own laws.

Immigration has to be solved because the presence of so many illegals has become a serious drain on our nation's resources, and that includes both the private and public sectors.

Now it's true that illegal aliens sometimes represent a cheap source of labor for certain kinds of employers, which explains why our friends at the U.S. Chamber of Commerce are not all that excited to see them deported. But we pay a price for that elsewhere. It's not so much about people losing their jobs to cheaper illegal labor, since a person who can do a better job is worth the additional wage and smart employers will understand that and pay it. But a flood of cheap, illegal workers distorts the labor force. Supply and demand applies to employment as with anything else, and people who are here illegally cause there to be too much supply, and that takes away some of the bargaining power of workers in general.

I don't mind the idea that people with the proper legal documentation might enter this country and join the workforce. That doesn't create a serious distortion and it won't cause talented American workers with solid skills to lose out on good jobs. But 12 million undocumented people are another story entirely.

And while people didn't like it when Donald Trump said it—that many illegal aliens are going to do a lot of other illegal things too—that taxes law enforcement, especially in border communities.

Solving this problem would seriously ease the pressure on our private- and public-sector resources, not to mention protecting the safety of people who are at risk of becoming crime victims because they happen to live in an area overrun by illegals. That's what makes it one of the right problems to deal with.

So how do we deal with it?

It starts with enforcing our existing laws. I hear a lot of talk about the need for "comprehensive immigration reform," which assumes that our existing immigration laws are an unworkable mess. But that's not true.

Let me give you a personal story that helps to demonstrate this. There is a young woman from South America who comes by our house every two weeks to help my wife, Gloria, clean the house. Recently she has been going through the official steps for citizenship. Contrary to what you might think, the process is not that complicated. It's not as if you have to submit 90 pages of paperwork. It's a fairly simple application.

But let me tell you what happened: After she submitted her paperwork, the ICE informed her that they had lost it. She spent months trying to track it down, and discovered it had gone to the wrong office, which promptly misplaced it. So after she did everything right and the government screwed it up, what did they tell her? They told her that she would have to start the process from the beginning.

That's just infuriating, but it's typical of how the federal government does things. And that leads me to this question: How can you say existing immigration laws don't work when a) they're not enforced; and b) the process is rife with incompetence?

By the way, you'll be glad to know that she persevered and was sworn in as a citizen in 2014. Good for her, because she followed the law and she didn't give up during the process!

When politicians talk about comprehensive immigration reform, what that usually means is that they want to make special rules for people who are already here—without tightening up the system we have. That makes no sense. We need to run ICE and INS better than they're run today. That alone would solve a lot of the problem. The reason so many illegal immigrants still continue to come to America is that the federal government does not effectively enforce the current immigration laws.

And of course, we need to secure the border, which doesn't necessarily require a wall from Texas to San Diego. Technology is available to help secure much of the border, although I would agree that a physical wall would be effective in certain spots. The combination of advanced surveillance and physical obstructions—along with enough manpower—could make our border essentially secure.

That would at least stop the growth of the problem, and we can start redirecting existing resources to finding and deporting those who shouldn't be here, and need to go back to their home countries and start the process of trying to come in legally—which, again, is not nearly as complicated as the "comprehensive immigration reform" people would have you believe.

Finally, these liberal cities who insist on being "sanctuary cities" that refuse to enforce immigration law need to be made to regret those policies. The federal government should withhold funding for housing, anti-blight and anything else that can be included for "sanctuary cities," and then we'll see how badly they want to protect these illegal aliens.

According to a recent article by Elizabeth Allen, an associate professor of English at UC Irvine, the American legal system is never perfectly responsive to people's circumstances, and sanctuary, while not included in our statutes, has often been invoked in the United States. In particular, groups who have been the subject of prejudicial laws have sought and used sanctuary, sometimes to evade what they considered to be an unfair law and sometime to issue broad public challenges to injustices within the legal system.[21]

The sanctuary cities of the 2000s are part of this American tradition. Some municipalities deliberately lay claim to the title explicitly to protect immigrants. Others simply wish to avoid potential legal problems that might stem from detaining people without full authority. Many, including Los Angeles, cite the difficulty of policing the city when the undocumented are afraid any contact with the authorities could end in deportation.[22]

Of course, the Obama administration could do this today if it was serious about enforcing existing law. And we all know perfectly well that it is not.

# CHAPTER 4

## THEN AGAIN, SOME THINGS JUST REQUIRE WILL AND WISDOM

### Four Problems We Can Solve Quickly Just By Embracing Better Public Policy

The four problems in this chapter are actually easier to solve, because they don't require the government to do anything other than make some different decisions. I would contrast that with, say, balancing the budget—which is one of the problems discussed in the previous chapter. It has to be done, but it's very difficult to achieve success. That's no excuse for failure; it's just recognition of the nature of the problem. I think we could balance the budget faster than the political class thinks we could do it, but I know we couldn't do it overnight.

The items in this chapter, though, can be accomplished just by someone deciding to do them. In that respect, the reality of these problems is both hopeful and infuriating. It's hopeful because it demonstrates that so much of what's required to put the country back on the right track is truly within our power to do. It's infuriating because it demonstrates the degree to which the political class has put us in this hole simply by refusing to do the right things.

But we can be infuriated all day long if we want. This book is all about solving problems and stewing over inaction is not going to solve the problem. So let's choose to be hopeful and recognize that we have the power to achieve these solutions if we will just embrace the wisdom and the will to do it.

These next four problems are just begging for the right leadership to address them:

### *Achieving True Energy Independence and Security*

You want to talk about a problem that's entirely of the federal government's making? This is it. There is absolutely no reason we should be dependent on foreign nations—especially those not particularly friendly to us—to supply us with the energy sources we need. America is rich with oil reserves, coal and natural gas. We are also more than capable of safely generating nuclear power.

We have the capacity to extract these resources, to refine them where necessary, and to distribute them throughout the country. We even have the capacity to make the whole enterprise highly profitable by exporting some of our resources across the globe—such that other nations are dependent on us for energy sources.

And all the federal government needs to do to make these things happen is change its policies. The market will take it from there and do the rest. These policies differ in that some are purely operating policies while others would require legislation to affect any change.

This is one of the right problems to solve for three crucially important reasons.

First, unleashing the full power of the energy reserves America has at the ready would dramatically and permanently reduce energy costs simply by virtue of its impact on supply. I realize that would also present a challenge for American producers in making a profit, because they would have to sell at lower prices. But that's the nature of competition. It's how markets are shaped. The producers who can operate efficiently enough, and can provide the type of service consumers want, will be successful at the price range set by the market. Those who can't, will not. If you think about what you spend every month filling your gas tank, heating your home, powering your electrical appliances and devices... then think about the impact of a major reduction in those costs. It would be like you got a raise or a tax cut. Now imagine the impact if everyone in

America got that raise or tax cut, not to mention the fact that more of the money they do spend on energy would be going to American companies rather than overseas.

Second, a real American commitment to energy production on a massive scale completely changes the dynamic that has long existed between the U.S. and other oil-producing countries. And that's a good thing. It puts us in a stronger position in those relationships. It means we need them less and we're in a stronger position to stand up for our interests. As it stands now, it's difficult for us to stand up against some of the emirs and potentates in the Middle East when they support terrorism and abuse human rights, because we need their oil. The same is true of Venezuela, which is limping along with a socialist economy and jailing political prisoners. Its oil revenue is the only thing keeping that regime afloat, and a lot of that money is coming from us because we have no choice but to buy what they're selling. That's insane. And keep in mind, bringing down global energy costs is also good for America because it weakens OPEC and other hostile nations who use jacked up oil prices to fund all kinds of things—including terrorism, in many cases—that are counter to our interests. The only reason OPEC is able to set the market at will—deciding when to pull back on production and when to boost it—is that we refuse to really get in the game to the extent we could.

Third, the potential for job creation in a truly unleashed American energy sector is enormous. And these wouldn't be make-work jobs like the ones politicians presume to create with "shovel-ready" projects and all that sort of nonsense. These would be permanent jobs that would give people the opportunity to do highly productive and very necessary work that creates value and wealth for the nation.

These are huge benefits, and the potential to realize them is greater than ever—especially now with the ascent of fracking. The technology to truly exploit our energy resources has advanced to the point where there is no longer even a plausible excuse (not that there ever really was) to resist the full-on pursuit of energy development in the United States.

Here are the policy changes the federal government needs to make in order to solve this problem and realize this vision:

First, cease and desist in the war on coal. Coal is the source of 40 percent of electricity in the United States,[1] and we've got 500 years' worth of it.[2] Yet the Obama administration is trying to kill the industry in a foolhardy attempt to force us into using green energy—which currently only provides about 7 percent of our electricity needs.[3]

Second, put the EPA on a leash, especially as it pertains to fracking. The administration has tried to scare people by implying that fracking is a threat to the environment—even trying to blame it for earthquakes—but the truth is they have no data to back up their claims that fracking is a threat of any kind. And they know it.[4]

Third, end the ban on oil exports. This was imposed in the 1970s during the darkest days of the oil embargo—when the government thought it would create an existential crisis if we let U.S.-produced oil out of the country. Like so many laws Congress passes, this stands today as a relic of a bygone era with no relevance to modern times. Let U.S. producers decide what to distribute domestically and what to export. That maximizes their economic power and maximizes the economic value of America's natural resources.

Fourth, relax the restrictions on new refineries and distribution of oil and gas throughout the U.S. This aspect of the business is much more expensive than it needs to be because politicians put up every barrier they can think of to it.

Fifth, stop using unfortunate but very rare oil spills as an excuse to stop off-shore drilling.

Sixth, sell the federal land on which there are major oil reserves just waiting to be extracted—but for the inability of producers to get leases from the federal government. There is no reason the federal government needs to own these lands. Sell them to energy developers and put the money toward principal on the national debt. Or do something else useful with it. But don't keep the land sitting there vacant and unproductive when the private sector can be turning it into energy resources and wealth.

Seventh, open up the Arctic National Wildlife Refuge to drilling. The ANWR consists of 19 million square miles, and it sits on a vast reserve of oil. The oil companies say they can get all the oil out of there if they are allowed to explore a mere 2,000 square miles—out of 19 million![5] There is no reason in the world not to let this happen.

Every single step I just recommended is a simple matter of the federal government changing policy. The rest happens naturally after that. That means we are dependent on other countries for energy today solely because of federal policy. That should not be allowed to remain true for one more day.

## *Dramatically Reduce Federal Regulations*

Federal regulations represent a major drag on the U.S. economy for a number of reasons, but the biggest reason is this: When a federal agency decides to impose a new regulation or rule, they are not required to come up with an economic justification for it. So they don't even try to determine if the rule is economically justified. Why should they? They just impose it because they want to, and they can.

During the Obama administration alone, federal agencies have issued more than 2,300 new regulations. These come from a variety of agencies and are often imposed without any type of congressional action. Agencies make rules that they say are necessary to enforce existing statutes, but there is no real constraint on these agencies' authority to impose these rules.

Not long ago, a bill was introduced in Congress that said any regulation that would have an impact of more than $100 million on a particular sector of the economy could not be imposed. It went nowhere, but this idea can't be allowed to go away. Congress has to put some sort of limits in place so a regulation-happy administration can't just use creative interpretations of statutes to impose whatever regulations it likes.

This is one of the right problems to address because federal regulations are a serious drag on the growth and prosperity of the private sector.

In an August 2014 report for Forbes, writer Kasia Moreno discussed a survey from Forbes Insights and KPMG that demonstrated just how impactful federal regulations are:[6]

The two sectors currently most affected by the regulatory environment in the U.S. are health care and financial services. In the financial sector, there are a number of regulatory mandates oriented toward transparency and reducing overall market risk. The sheer quantity of regulations coming at financial services companies can be hard to grasp.

New regulations are expensive in terms of compliance, as companies need to transform data tracking and gathering systems, reporting functions and, in some cases, their organizational structures. At the same time, these regulations can limit revenue growth and profitability by, for example, increasing capital ratio requirements and limiting certain products or activities.

Prosperity Bank's chairman and CEO, David Zalman, puts the current regulatory environment in perspective: "I've been in banking since 1978, and today, probably over half of my time is spent with regulatory requirements. The regulatory burden is a threat to traditional community banking. It is troubling that we don't always know what the regulators are going to want."

Other industries, such as energy, are also affected by a strong regulatory component. PG&E's chief executive, Anthony Earley, can personally identify with the focus on the regulatory issues. "A constructive regulatory environment can either help or hurt us. I absolutely spend time with state and federal regulators. As CEO, most of my time is spent on regulatory issues."

Is it a good idea for U.S. CEOs to devote so much of their time to regulatory issues? They have no choice, and the regulatory burdens are not lessening anytime soon. "The global pace of regulatory change is accelerating," says Tim Zuber, regulatory center leader at KPMG. Complying with regulations generally creates a drag on businesses. Regulatory compliance can add costs, slow down processes and restrict expansion.

Considering that the CEOs and their organizations already focus on the regulatory issues, it makes sense to derive value out of new regulatory compliance processes. "One way to do so is to take data and insights that in the past have been used almost exclusively for compliance purposes and use them to drive additional value," says Zuber.

For example, sales data required solely for indirect tax compliance purposes may be analyzed to provide new or better insights on product and customer profitability that otherwise was not known or knowable. With these insights, better decision making outside of the tax function may be possible. In fact, the regulatory environment is so impactful that in highly regulated industries companies are changing their business models as a result of regulations.

When CEOs are spending more time working to comply with regulations than they are generating profits, it should be abundantly clear that the regulatory state is out of control. Perhaps this doesn't strike the political class as particularly problematic, since to them compliance with federal rules probably is a higher priority than private sector profits. And that's the very reason these people shouldn't have so much power over the rest of us.

New leaders in Washington need to go through the federal register and get rid of every federal regulation for which they can't come up with a compelling reason and a strong economic justification, then pass new laws very clearly restricting the freedom of federal agencies from imposing new ones.

### Rebuilding Our Military

This is a task that takes good leadership and good management skill—something that is admittedly not that easy to come by in Washington—but it's first and foremost just a choice someone has to make about spending priorities. Is national defense and national security the first responsibility of the federal government? I believe it is. I think most people do. And if that's the case, then we need to decide what this costs and allocate it before we commit one more dime of the federal budget to anything else.

Why does this make the list of the right problems? Because America's global strategic interests are crucially important, and we are in a much weaker position to pursue these interests when our military is a) not fully capable; or b) led by people unwilling to act.

New leadership alone can solve the latter problem. But the former will require serious money and commitment. And can anyone seriously doubt that we need to do this? Eastern Europe is under threat from Russia. ISIS is running wild in the Middle East. Iran is pursuing the bomb, and instead of asserting our strategic superiority to stop them, the administration actually negotiated the deal that will make it happen! Uprisings in Syria and Libya have turned into disasters, in part because America can't decide what it wants to do or what it can do. The war in Afghanistan now drags into a 15th year, and anything resembling decisive victory seems little more than a pipe dream at this point. Under this administration, they simply do not have a sound strategy for dealing with these conflicts.

And it's not just because President Obama is unwilling to act, although that is certainly true. He has also decimated the military to the point where we can't do nearly as much as we might need to do.

According to a recent report from the Heritage Foundation:

- The Army is shrinking from 570,000 soldiers to 440,000 at most.
- The Navy no longer has a 300-ship force. There is actually talk of having our sailors hitch rides on other nations' ships. The current size of the fleet is only 284, which is 62 short of the force we would need to carry out two large campaigns.[7]
- While Heritage says we would need 50 brigades to carry out two major campaigns, the Army currently has only 33 brigades.

Right now we are retro-fitting old ground combat vehicles rather than ordering new ones.

Why has this all happened? It's happened because Obama has cut Pentagon spending—not counting the cost of overseas conflicts—to under $500 billion a year.

By the way, don't overlook the threat of cyberattacks and the military's need to be ready for those. I met not long ago with General Stanley MacChrystal so he could fill me in on the seriousness of this threat. He told me that our energy grids are very vulnerable to an attack that could virtually shut down this country with a simple computer virus.

Now what if an enemy could do that to our military? We can't afford to have that happen.

I realize some will see this as contradicting my other priorities, especially the one about balancing the budget, because rebuilding our military will undoubtedly require us to spend more than we're spending now. Some will even see it as hypocritical. I've heard liberals say things like, 'Oh, you conservatives love cutting the budget until it comes to the military!'

Well, yes. I'm not sure why they think that's a criticism. The federal government needs to be very good at the functions that it and only it can do. National defense is clearly one of those functions. In order for the military to be able to do its job with excellence, it needs enough resources, which means not misallocating the limited resources we have to things that do not deserve such a high priority status.

So, yes, I want more spending on the military and less on most other things. And new leaders for our nation need to embrace the same priority for the same reasons.

## Enforce Our Constitution and Laws

This should be obvious. How can something as basic as this belong on a list of the right problems America needs to urgently address? That's a great question, and it's precisely because it should be so basic that it's become such a big problem.

Because it isn't happening.

When Americans can't be confident that their basic laws and constitutional structures will be respected by those elected to federal office, every reason we have for confidence in our elected and appointed officials breaks down.

A few years ago, a Democratic congressman named Fortney "Pete" Stark from California opined that in this day and age, the federal government can pretty much do whatever it wants. That, of course, is completely wrong—in theory. The Constitution was written very specifically to limit the powers of the federal government vis-à-vis the states and the people, and furthermore to limit the powers of any one branch of the federal government vis-à-vis the others. That is to prevent tyranny.

But it only works if those we elect under this system respect it and follow it. Let me give you four examples of where this has broken down:

In the 2012 case NFIB v. Sebelius, a majority on the Supreme Court agreed that the federal government did not have the authority to fine people if they did not buy health insurance.[8] That, you'd think, would have been a fatal blow to ObamaCare. But instead, Chief Justice John Roberts essentially re-wrote the law by calling the fine a "tax" and then declared this constitutional. The Supreme Court's job was to decide if the law was constitutional or not, and if it wasn't, to get rid of it. Instead, the chief justice decided his priority was to find a way to save it by calling a part of it something it clearly is not.

In 2013, the Obama administration unilaterally decided not to enforce the employer mandate in ObamaCare even though the statutory language clearly spelled out the date by which the mandate must be enforced. Neither Congress nor the judiciary did anything to challenge this.

In 2014, President Obama announced he would not enforce deportation laws against illegal aliens. Congress threatened to withhold funding from the Department of Homeland Security in an attempt to force the president to enforce the law, but when faced with another "shutdown showdown," Congress folded like a cheap suit. The law is still not being enforced.[9]

In the 2015 case King v. Burwell, the Supreme Court again saved ObamaCare as a majority led (once again) by Chief Justice Roberts ruled that even though the law clearly says health insurance premiums can only be subsidized if they are bought on an exchange "established by the State," the law can't possibly mean that because it wouldn't work if it did.

Laws mean things. The Constitution means things. The Obama administration doesn't care what the law or the Constitution mean, and why should they? Congress won't stand up to them and neither will the Supreme Court. The media won't criticize them for abusing their power. So they just do whatever they want.

This means the end of any accountability or openness in government. If you can't trust your elected officials to operate within the limits of their power, and you can't trust the other branches of government to see to it that they do, what accountability is left for those in government?

There is none. If the next round of leaders we elect don't get this under control, then our representative form of government ceases to mean anything.

# CHAPTER 5

## RESTORATION OF NATIONAL PRIDE

It's Amazing What Solving Problems
Can Do for a Nation's Psyche

One of the most important benefits of solving the nine problems discussed in the two previous chapters is also one of the least tangible. But anyone who really understands leadership knows that it's vital. It's the restoration of America's national pride.

Now I'm not saying that you, as you read this book, no longer feel pride about being an American. You very well may. I know I do. But just because many (or even most) individuals feel pride in being Americans, that doesn't mean national pride as a whole is still what it should be.

National pride has taken a hit in recent years, and the tangible result of that waning pride is that it's much more difficult to get Americans behind big ideas and positive visions for what the country can do.

There is no doubt in my mind that America's capacity to do great things is stronger than ever. But your capacity doesn't do you any good if you don't believe in it, and I do not think Americans believe in their country's ability to do great things like we once did.

That starts with leadership. One of the first things Barack Obama did when he became president was to travel to other countries and apologize for America. It was a disgusting display. He went around and told the leaders of other nations that America had been too arrogant. He told regimes who had done—and were still doing— terrible things that America had no room to talk because we had done our own terrible things.

When asked if he believed in American exceptionalism, he said, "I believe in American exceptionalism, just as I'm sure the Brits believe in British exceptionalism and the Greeks believe in Greek exceptionalism."

In other words, no, he doesn't. Exceptionalism means that you consider your nation exceptional—one of a kind. If every country is exceptional, then there's no such thing as exceptionalism. Clearly, this is Obama's view of our nation. He believes we are nothing all that special, and that we have had too haughty a view of ourselves vis-à-vis the rest of the world.

No organization can ever rise above the limitations of its leader, and that goes for nations too. How can a nation not take a hit to its national pride when its own leader takes such a dim view of it?

Another reason national pride is suffering is the palpable sense people get that we can't solve our problems. We can't get serious economic growth going again. We can't get the work force back to full strength. We can't deal with our entitlement problems. We can't stem the tide of moral degradation. We can't end our energy dependence. We can't exercise leadership around the world.

Now in truth, it's not that we can't. It's that we have leaders who won't. But we also have a majority of the electorate that keeps electing these do-nothing leaders, which causes those who are concerned about these problems to lose faith in their fellow countrymen.

Among other problems, this makes anti-American ideologues feel more confident in their pronouncements. I had a caller to my radio show in June 2015 who was upset because his daughter, a college student, had just been told by her professor that her vote doesn't really count. (Tell that to the 500-odd voters in Florida who decided the 2000 presidential election.) So why would a college professor say something like this? Because it's his way of running down the country and its democratic traditions. It's his way of attacking the national pride of a young woman who had always been told her vote was valuable, because she lived in a nation that empowers its citizens.

No, he told her, you don't really have any power as a citizen in America.

If she had believed that, what a sucker punch in the gut to her national pride! But that's what you get when you're constantly having to listen to the voices of people who view America like Obama does!

So if you're going to restore national pride, where does that start? We really shouldn't find that to be such a mystery, because it wasn't that long ago that we faced the same challenge. If you're old enough to remember the 1980 election, you'll recall that American pride had hit rock bottom during the presidency of Jimmy Carter. There were a lot of reasons for that, some of which related to Carter's own inability to project hope and optimism. He once even chastised the country for having fallen into a "national malaise" (as if he had nothing to do with it).

But there were also tangible reasons for Americans to be down in the dumps. Inflation was running wild. Interest rates were approaching 20 percent. Unemployment was on the rise. And Americans were being held hostage by the ayatollahs in Iran, with the U.S. government seemingly helpless to do anything but engage in fruitless negotiations.

When Ronald Reagan swept to victory in November 1980 and took office the following January, he immediately projected a sense of hope and optimism that we hadn't seen for some time. Americans believed that he meant the things he said, and would do the things he said he would do. (The Iranians certainly believed it. They released the hostages the day Reagan took office.)

But it was one thing to project a sense of optimism. Reagan had always been able to do that. He was, after all, an actor. But it was quite another thing to get about the work of solving the problems. And when Americans saw Reagan doing that with a vengeance, the entire sense of what it meant to be an American started to change—and started to take on a veneer of pride we hadn't seen in quite some time.

We got interest rates under control. We tamed inflation. We weathered a deep recession and then the economy started growing again. Like crazy. We did more. We rebuilt our military. We stood up to the Soviet Union around the globe.

A particular moment that defined this period for many came in 1985, after Middle Eastern hijackers had taken control of a cruise ship in the Mediterranean and murdered an elderly American named Leon Klinghoffer—whose body they unceremoniously dumped overseas while his horrified wife watched. The hijackers had arranged for a getaway plane, and once the plane came to get them it appeared they might never be apprehended.

But not so fast. President Reagan ordered U.S. fighter jets to scramble and bring down the getaway plane, and we arrested the hijackers. The next day's headline in the New York Daily News summed it up: "WE BAG THE BUMS."[1]

That's the way America was at that time. We believed we could solve problems. Stand up to foes. Refuse to take 'no' for an answer. And that came so soon after the "national malaise" for which President Carter just couldn't seem to find the solution.

What Reagan understood that Carter didn't was that the answer was leadership. It was action. It was resolve. You want to convince people that America can do good things? Great things? Big things? Worthy things? Then take the reins and do them. Don't take a poll. Don't check with your political consultant. Make the kind of decision a leader would make, and take action.

Solving the problems I outlined in the previous two chapters would serve as a powerful restoration of national pride.

- Imagine if we led the world in energy production. We could.
- Imagine if we balanced our budget every year without drama. It's very doable.
- Imagine businesses free to grow and prosper without harassment from regulators. Why not?
- Imagine calculating your taxes with a simple formula and paying a reasonable amount, which is the same simple percentage everyone else pays. That could be reality.
- Imagine the world's bad actors once again afraid to challenge us. It can happen.

- Imagine the poor and elderly secure in their retirement and their health without bankrupting the government in the process. We can do this.

Imagine leaders who respect our constitution and laws. Let's elect some!

An America that has achieved all this would beam with pride. People would live with more confidence. People would be more willing to sacrifice for their country. People would be more willing to trust their leaders, and the trust would be rewarded.

I want to pose a question to every one of you: Do you want to live in an America like this, or do you want to live in Rick Santorum's America? Now I'm sure you're wondering right about now why I'm picking on fellow Republican Rick Santorum. I'll tell you why:

During my 2012 run for the presidency, Santorum was asked what he thought of my                    .
9-9-9 plan. He said, "It would never pass."

I have never forgotten that. The political class in this country deals in the realm of what "can pass," not of what will solve the problem. And that goes for Republicans and Democrats alike. As we'll discuss in detail in the next chapter, many of them don't even want to solve these problems. It's more in their personal and political interests to leave the problems unsolved.

So do you want to live in an America where we do what can pass? Or where we do what will work? Because if you choose the former, I'm not surprised that you're struggling a bit with your national pride. But for those who choose the latter, I say stop taking 'no' for an answer from our leaders and elect leaders who will say 'yes.' That's how we get back to an America that can once again make us all proud.

# CHAPTER 6

## FRIENDS OF THE STATUS QUO

### Why the Political Class Doesn't Want To Solve the Problems That Really Matter

If the right problems are the things we discussed in Chapters 3 and 4, that seems to beg a fairly obvious question: Why don't our leaders solve these problems?

And the answer is fairly straightforward: They don't want to.

To examine that in more detail, let's consider who we're talking about. When we use the term "political class," that consists of several groups of people. It's politicians, of course, but it's also political consultants, lobbyists, government employees and the media who cover politics.

I am sure that within this group of people, there are individuals who want to solve problems. But the culture of each group is to resist real solutions because they perceive (often correctly) that it is more in their personal self-interest to maintain the status quo.

Let's explore this by looking at the perspectives of a few different groups so we can understand why they really don't want to solve problems. We'll consider:

- Republican politicians
- Democrat politicians
- Political consultants
- Lobbyists
- Government employees
- The political media

Each group has its own agenda, and while you will get the occasional individual who serves as an outlier within that group, the groupthink cannot be reversed by those individuals because there simply are not enough of them.

### *Republican politicians*

For conservatives, this is the most maddening group to consider because these are the people we think (or at least hope) will work toward real solutions. These are the people who voice support for conservative policy positions when they campaign. These are the people who so often give you the impression they understand the folly of liberal policies.

So why, once they get into office, don't they solve the problems?

Consider the Congress we had between 2002 and 2006. Republicans not only held the White House but the House and the Senate as well. It was the perfect opportunity to do some crucially important things. They could have:

- Replaced the tax code with a simpler, fairer system with low rates
- Gotten federal spending under control
- Instituted market-based reforms to healthcare finance
- Opened up greater domestic energy production, particularly in the Arctic
- Restructured entitlement programs with more emphasis on the role of the private sector
- Slashed business regulations
- Ended the political manipulation of the currency

Not a single Democrat vote would have been required to do any of this. A Republican Congress and a Republican president could have made them the law. So why didn't they?

It's easy to say that they're all RINOs (Republicans In Name Only for those of you who don't trade in conservative jargon on a daily basis), but there's more going on than that.

Money in politics is driven by those who are most invested in political outcomes. Now that might seem obvious, but consider the question: As opposed to whom? Who doesn't have that much invested in political outcomes? The answer is people whose well-being don't really depend all that much on politics.

If you own a small business and you sell products and services to the public, you're not asking the government to do all that much for you. You probably want them to stay out of your way as much as anything else. You want your tax bill to be as low as possible, and you want the regulators to leave you alone. But you don't need any special favors from government.

For that reason, you're probably a conservative, but you're also probably not going to spend big money to influence the outcome of an election because the success of your business doesn't depend on it. It might be harder if a Democrat wins, but your success doesn't depend on what the government does so you could overcome that if you had to.

But for many big businesses, it's a different story. A certain trade bill or regulatory action could be the difference between their survival or their demise. A change in interest rates could cripple them. The elimination of a given subsidy might impact a crucial market they serve.

Big businesses who have invested millions in lobbyists and campaign contributions aren't necessarily looking for a radical change in the way government operates. Why? Because they've learned to play the game. They've learned how to make big government work to their benefit. They've learned how to influence regulatory policy so it helps them and hurts their competitors.

And they depend on their representatives and senators to assist them in these efforts. A very principled conservative who refuses to manipulate public policy to the benefit of an important constituent is going to hear the following: How can you not do it for us when all your colleagues do it for their constituents?

Business and community leaders in a given area can also be examples of conservative principles that go only so far. Rail against out-of-control government spending and they'll cheer you on. As long as you're only talking in the abstract. But their bike trail, or their research hospital, or their preschool program, or their historic preservation prospect... that's worthy! And it's usually not the Granola-eating, Birkenstock-wearing, tie-dyed hippies in the community who are asking their congressman to get them this money from Washington. It's the Chamber of Commerce board, consisting of leading manufacturers and lawyers and real estate agents. They too have spent years learning to play the game, and they know how to play it better than a lot of other people.

They don't want to lose that advantage.

Now, they might want to elect Republicans. But that doesn't mean they want to give up all the advantages they've won for themselves.

Take the insurance industry, for example. Do they want to elect Democrats? Absolutely not. Democrats beat them up all the time. But what they do want is public policy that causes more people to purchase their services. Health insurers have enjoyed an advantage for years because the federal government gives a tax deduction for employer-purchased health insurance. This tax policy really doesn't make sense and hasn't for decades, but tell a Republican to get rid of it and that Republican will hear from the insurance lobby, which will apply major pressure to keep it in place.

Or consider an auto insurer. They may want to elect Republicans in the hope they can get policies that will limit their liability in offering coverage. But do they want to see small-government policies that might give people the choice whether to purchase or not purchase their product? No way.

The occasional principled Republican will resist this kind of pressure. But most will take the path of least resistance and support their powerful constituencies' interest in playing the game.

I will admit that I didn't understand this earlier in my career. When I first became president of the National Restaurant Association, I was very interested (as I am now) in seeing the tax code replaced. It seemed natural to me that we could gain an ally in the U.S. Chamber of Commerce, since I figured their members would be equally interested in both reducing and simplifying the burden imposed on them by the tax code.

So I scheduled a meeting with the Chamber's governmental affairs chief, confident that he would be enthusiastic about my proposal and about the prospect that we could work together on it. To put it mildly, that is not what happened. As I sat and explained why I thought the tax code should be thrown out and be replaced, I realized he was shifting quite uncomfortably, looking at me like I was from another planet. He never really explained his objection to the idea, but it was clear just from the tone of the conversation that the Chamber wouldn't be interested in working with us on this issue.

I couldn't figure out why at the time, but I know why now. The Chamber and other major interest groups have figured out how to make big, complicated government work for its members. They are the ones who steer their members through the maze. It's one of the reasons they're needed. It's really not in their interest to solve this or many other problems, because their members depend on them to manage the problems.

So the Republican establishment isn't that motivated to solve these problems because their biggest supporters are people who have learned how to do quite well as the problems persist. Solving the problems would render much of the establishment structure unnecessary, and what would they do then? That's why the goal of Republicans is usually to get control of big government and run it in a Republican-friendly way.

I will never forget, when I was leading the polls for the 2012 Republican presidential nomination and my 9-9-9 plan was much in the news, Rick Santorum offered the following criticism of it: "That would never pass."

That was a criticism, all right—but of the political class, not of 9-9-9. We'll never solve anything if we only propose what "can pass" rather than what will actually work. But there was truth to what he said. If I had succeeded and replaced the tax code with 9-9-9, the entire political establishment would have lost a good deal of its power— including the Republican establishment. That is one of the biggest reasons they did not want me to succeed.

Back to that Republican-dominated era of 2002-2006, then: Why didn't they solve those problems? Because their primary supporters are comfortable with the status quo. They might want it tweaked at the margins, but they don't want it thrown out and replaced because then they would have no advantage over the average person who does not have a lot of political connections, and who does not spend big money on politics.

It's easier to get along by going along. It avoids controversy and saves you from criticism. And that's how most politicians want it—including Republicans.

### *Democrat politicians*

For a Democrat, the motivation to leave problems unsolved is different, although it's similar to Republicans' reasons in that it is certainly connected to self-interest. But it's connected to ideology too.

Most Democrats have idealistic, stars-in-the-eyes notions of what government is capable of. They really believe that government can solve every problem, right every wrong, correct every injustice. What's more, they believe that anyone who doesn't want government to be the primary problem-solver doesn't want the problem solved at all, because only government can really achieve results.

I know that goes against every bit of historical evidence when you look at what's actually happened, but to a liberal, if government failed it just means government didn't have enough money, enough support from the public, or enough acceptance from Republicans. It's like the people who say communism didn't fail because real communism was never really tried. They're the true believers and their faith is unshakable.

So how does this prove that they don't want problems solved?

This gets to the other thing you have to understand about Democrats. The political/big government world is the world they know. It's the world they're comfortable operating in. Remember the scene in Ghostbusters when the guys have been thrown out of the university, their funding revoked? Bill Murray's character Peter Venkman figures the Ghostbusters can just go into business for themselves. Dan Aykroyd's Ray Stantz replies, with an unmistakable dread in his voice, "In the private sector, they expect results!"

And that's exactly the point. The private sector expects results. The public sector just expects you to keep doing what you do. The government and the nonprofit world consist of agencies and departments and offices and divisions and boards and commissions who have been around for decades (if not centuries), ostensibly for the purpose of solving some problem or addressing some need. In reality, the problems are no closer to being solved than on the day these institutions were created, but they just keep on keeping on. And they've gotten very good at justifying their own existence with rhetorical arguments.

No, poverty isn't any better than it was when the War on Poverty started. But just think how much worse it would be without it!

No, we're not more energy-independent than we were before we established the Department of Energy. But we'd be in even bigger trouble without it!

No, education hasn't improved since the Department of Education was created. But imagine how terrible things would be if the federal government didn't play a role!

These arguments make no sense, of course, but they don't need to. This isn't the private sector. You don't have to produce results. You just have to produce arguments that the right politicians can sell to the right bloc of voters so they will stay in office and keep funding you.

A classic example is the relationship between Democrats and public employee unions. It's one of the most corrupt circles you can ever imagine. Just look at recent situations in which the IRS, the DEA and the Veterans Administration discovered that their employees were guilty of horrendous conduct, but almost no one responsible was fired. The agency heads explain that their hands are tied because of the union contracts, and that's exactly how the unions design it. They also make sure to elect people who will keep it that way. The unions contribute money to Democrat candidates, and once they're elected these Democrats give the public employees whatever they want in terms of wages, benefits and pension guarantees. And the next election cycle, the whole thing repeats.

This is the dynamic that bankrupted Detroit and is about to do the same thing in Chicago, but politicians resist changing it because it's the same dynamic that's been keeping them in office for generations.

Solving the problems we're talking about in this book would take away Democrats' power to exercise political control over many aspects of American life and, without that power, they couldn't deliver the rewards they constantly promise their constituents. Especially when you're predisposed to believe no problem can ever really be solved unless government solves it, these people are never going to let that happen.

### Political consultants

Behind every successful campaign is a very good consultant, and in the abstract there is nothing wrong with that. But consultants don't like their candidates to talk about things that don't poll well, or that might engender controversy, or that might open up a line of criticism from an opponent.

That being the case, there are certain ideas that will send consultants running through the halls screaming that the world is coming to an end. One is to suggest that Social Security should be touched in any way. I can tell you that Social Security is not as fiscally sound as the political class tries to pretend it is, and a lot of candidates understand it needs to be restructured.

But your consultant doesn't want you to say a word about that in a campaign because your opponent will accuse you of wanting to make Grandma sleep under a highway overpass and eat dog food. It doesn't matter that this is nonsense. It doesn't matter that not solving the problem will probably result in that very thing at some point. All that matters is that your consultant doesn't want to be on the defensive end of a difficult news cycle between now and Election Day.

Why does this matter? It matters because governing effectively requires the consent of the governed, and if no one will campaign on real solutions to real problems, then they will not have the support of the public to implement those solutions once they are in office.

There is another reason political consultants don't want problems solved, and this is that they've become very comfortable with the rhetoric of the status quo. Watch any talking-head battle on cable news between a Republican strategist and a Democrat strategist. It's very easy to predict the talking points and insults they'll toss back and forth because they've practiced it for years. They like the political world the way it is today. They're the masters of it. Change it, and they have to learn all new strategies and all new talking points.

Also, any real problem solver who gets elected is going to do it by ignoring their advice, and if that happens, what will that do to them?

## *Lobbyists*

This may be the easiest one to explain. Lobbyists don't want problems solved because that's not their job. Their job is to work the existing system to the benefit of their clients. The tax code is a complicated mess but they know how to get just the right exemption passed to benefit their clients. The budget is out of control, but that means there's lots of money being spent and they know how to make sure that the people who pay them a handsome retainer keep getting their share. The regulators are impossible to deal with, but don't worry, because your lobbyist can make sure they don't give you a hard time.

You can expand this to a lot of consultant classes. Ask your tax consultant if the tax code is an oppressive behemoth, and he'll tell you it absolutely is. Ask him if he'd like to see it replaced by something like the FairTax or 9-9-9. Not a chance! Because if that happened, what would you need him for?

Those former IRS agents who advertise on TV for their services in helping you to get your tax debt reduced? The ones who tell you how awful the IRS is? Do you think they want the IRS to go away? Absolutely not. They need the IRS to be exactly the horrible way it is so you will need them to help you deal with it.

When something is almost impossible to deal with, the people who have learned how to deal with it have a lot of power. Once the thing becomes easy for everyone to deal with, that is no longer the case.

### Political media

Do you know what makes the stars of the political media important? Do you know why they can command so much money for what they do? Because when government is so influential over everyone's lives, the people who presume to explain it to you are some of the most important information sources you will ever have.

If everyone's job security depends on what the president says about the economy today, then the people who bring us that news are famous and influential. If everyone's health depends on a policy that comes out of Washington, then we'll tune in with unbridled attention to hear from the reporters who can tell us that information.

The media is very government-centric, and that's true at every level. As we discussed in Chapter 2, the plum assignment at any local newspaper is never the business beat. It's always City Hall, or the Capitol. Those are the assignments reporters work their way up to. The ones considered by editors to be the very best in the field are given those beats.

And because of that culture, the prevailing thought in the media world is that government is where the action is. When a person runs for office, the media want to know how they would use the power of government to solve people's problems. If you tell a reporter that you think people should solve their own problems, you're not going to get very favorable coverage.

And over time, political reporters cultivate all kinds of sources within government. They know who to call at the Pentagon, the State Department, or the Department of Agriculture, to get the information they need. They learn the ins and outs of things like Freedom of Information Act Requests, and of how you go about covering a public meeting. They are not part of the government, but they are very much creatures of it.

So if government becomes less influential, so do they—not to mention the fact that they have to start re-learning everything they know.

There is also this: Journalists are extremely cynical. Again, there are exceptions, but prevailing culture within journalism is a highly cynical one—and that leads most journalists to believe it's not even possible to solve problems, assuming they could even find a sincere politician who really wanted to solve them (and of course they do not believe that).

So what you have here is a perfect storm of devotion to the status quo.

Republicans don't want to solve problems because their biggest supporters like things the way they are.

Democrats don't want to solve the problems because they prefer to just perpetually manage the problems.

Consultants don't want to let candidates even talk about real solutions because that will cause controversy and falling poll numbers.

Lobbyists don't want to see problems solved because their job is to guide their clients around the problems everyone else has to deal with.

And the press won't hold anyone accountable for solving problems because they don't believe in solutions anyway—especially if they involve a lessening of the role of government.

Is there any way to solve this? There is. The solution is real leadership.

# CHAPTER 7

## LEADERSHIP... IT STARTS AT THE TOP

### What Real, Difference-Making
### Leadership Looks Like

As I write this book about working on the right problems and coming up with the right solutions, I can hear the groans of the consultant class and the political media, proclaiming: That's never going to happen!

And while they're certainly not right to say it can never happen, they are correct in the sense that they're accurately gauging the culture of Washington. That's why we spent so much time in the previous chapter looking at the various groups in Washington who don't want to solve these problems—and why. This is indeed the reality of the culture that permeates the federal government, and sets the parameters for the entire political class in defining what can be done.

It would be tempting, therefore, to declare that these proposed solutions are unrealistic, and that it would be better to abandon them in favor of more realistic goals. You know, stuff that can pass. The problem with that, of course, is that stuff that can pass isn't the stuff that will solve the problems. So if you want to solve the problems, you need to change the culture.

And that requires real leadership.

When a new leader comes into an organization and needs to change its fortunes, one of the biggest mistakes he can make is to think, "I need to get to know the culture so I can fit into it." No. When an organization is failing, the culture is almost always part of the problem—if not the main problem. What an effective leader needs to do is get a sense of the culture so he can recognize where it needs to change.

Then he has to make sure he changes it.

Now a lot of people probably imagine that leaders change organizational cultures by giving stirring, inspirational speeches that motivate everyone to change what they do and how they do it. This is where Barack Obama serves as a good object lesson. I never much cared for the substance of his speeches, but you had to recognize during his campaign (if much less so during his presidency) that he had a real oratorical gift. Those who were aligned with him ideologically were excited about the way Obama spoke, and imagined that this would enable him to bring about a real change in the way the federal government operated.

Obviously, it didn't. So why is that? Anyone with real leadership experience knows the answer. Obama can talk all day long, but he doesn't have the slightest idea how to get people and organizations to change or improve their performance. He doesn't know how to back up his words with action. I think Obama really thought everyone would do things differently just because he sounded so good making speeches about it.

Real organizational leadership doesn't work that way.

When I was assigned by Pillsbury to take over as vice president/general manager of the Philadelphia region of Burger King, it was crucial that I recognize—and quickly— the things I could change that would make a difference. In the franchising business, you don't have the freedom to change everything, and you can't use that as an excuse not to get results. You can't change the menu, the ingredients, the operation standards or the content of the marketing. That's all determined at the corporate level.

But you can change the priorities that are emphasized in leading the organization. And you can get people thinking differently about what it takes to succeed. One thing I noticed right off the bat was that employees came to work in a funk—viewing it as a boring job they only did because they had to—and that attitude manifested in the service they gave the customers. If you came into a Burger King in this region, you could probably expect basic, bare-bones, mediocre service. You certainly weren't going to get anything better than that.

I had to teach the employees why excellent service was so important, and how it could change the performance of the business. I also had to develop some tools to help drive that message home. Because they knew I meant it, and because I gave them what they needed to make the change, performance in the region started to turn around. Once people could see the change in the results, the culture started changing too. They no longer believed service wasn't important. They realized service was critical. We then developed in-store reminders that the goal was to deliver "exceptional" service.

This was the part we could change. People still got the same Whopper and fries. They still came and ate in the same building. Being a franchise operation, we couldn't have changed those things if we'd wanted to. But customers noticed they were getting better service, and the metrics proved it was driving better business results.

A change in an organization's culture doesn't have to happen in multiple dimensions. Sometimes a serious change in one crucial area can do it. But it has to start with the leader, and the leader has to both equip his people to make the change and hold them accountable for achieving it.

When I then moved on to Godfather's Pizza, there was more than one problem. The three major issues were product quality, service and cleanliness. These are fundamentals of any successful restaurant operation, and Godfather's wasn't doing well at any of them.

Let me give you a couple of examples from the realm of product quality. There's a technique called "proofing" a crust. You use what's called a proofing rack, and the crust is supposed to sit on it for 30 minutes so it can fluff up and become a bit more tender. Not only did the employees routinely skip the proofing process, but most of the stores didn't even have proofing racks.

I also discovered people were cutting corners when it came to toppings. If a recipe called for 12 pepperonis on a pizza, employees would use just 10. They figured the customers wouldn't notice. The customers noticed.

So I went to work setting new standards for product quality, service and cleanliness. A few times I had to raise hell because I caught someone not proofing a crust. A few times I fired people. That was no fun, but this was how they knew I was serious. And as the word started to spread that I was serious the culture of the organization changed—and just like with Burger King in Philadelphia, so did the results.

When it came to cleanliness, I made it clear that I didn't want clean restaurants. I wanted immaculate restaurants. That eliminated people applying their own definitions of what clean might be. There is only one definition of immaculate, and if you missed anything, it's not immaculate. I needed to raise the standard that high to change the culture.

Another thing we needed to do at Godfather's was update the décor. Godfather's was founded in 1973. I took it over in

1986. If you remember those two decades, you know that the look of 1973 was pretty out of place in 1986. So I worked with the franchise owners to achieve an update to the look.

There was one guy, though, who just stubbornly refused to cooperate with the décor update. He owned just about all the franchise stores in the Denver market, and he made it clear to me and to everyone else who would listen that he wasn't remodeling anything. He didn't care what I said. He "wasn't going to remodel a damn thing," but he still expected me to pull a rabbit out of my hat and turn the company around.

Well, we did get much better results companywide, but this guy's stores in Denver weren't doing so well. I also learned he wasn't following my lead on service or cleanliness. Now in the franchise game, you can't just fire a franchisee. He owned the franchises and he had to live with the consequences of his choices.

So I wasn't surprised at all when he came to me six months later, struggling, and asking for royalty relief from the corporation. I asked him again if he'd remodeled the restaurants as the corporation had directed. No. I asked if he had enforced the quality and cleanliness standards we'd established. No. And yet he still expected me to lower his royalty rates so he could continue to operate according to the old culture.

I told him no. He had to file for bankruptcy and ultimately ended up selling all his restaurants out of bankruptcy.

Now I didn't enjoy making that decision. But if I had granted this guy his request, I would have been making one of the classic mistakes that leaders often make when they're trying to change organizational culture. If I had bailed out this guy in spite of his refusal to meet the standards I set, then everyone in the organization would have known that my standards didn't mean anything. I would have affirmed that everyone was free to operate according to the old standards, and that there would be no price to pay for doing so.

When I ran for president, some people thought it was pretty funny that a guy who ran a pizza joint (as some liked to put it) thought he could be president of the United States. This from people who voted for Barack Obama, who had never run anything.

In addition to the policy ideas I believed in and still do, I believed my experience qualified me for the job because of what I had learned about leading organizations and changing cultures. And if you don't think that's important, you need only look again to an example provided by Ronald Reagan.

Early in Reagan's first term, the Professional Air Traffic Controllers Organization (PATCO) decided to take its members out on strike. These were federal employees and they were prohibited by federal law from striking. But the union bosses had learned from years of experience that if they thumbed their noses at that law, they would be made to pay no price. No president would risk firing the PATCO workers and having to bring in an entirely new set of controllers.

Everything about the established culture of the federal government suggested PATCO could get away with this illegal strike. But Ronald Reagan was a different kind of president. Without hesitation, Reagan stunned the nation by firing the air traffic controllers. He then acted quickly to bring in new controllers so that air traveler safety would not be jeopardized.

The union bosses couldn't believe it. No president had ever stood up to them like this. But Reagan understood there was more at stake than just the short-term disruption his action might cause. He was trying to change the culture of the federal government, and that had to start by letting federal employees know that they couldn't just ignore the law. He had to establish that there would be a price to pay if they didn't do what was expected of them.

And boy, did he.

Now here's a secret that union bosses never admit, but it's undeniable. They didn't like Reagan, and they were angry about many of his policies. But they respected him. They knew he was an adversary they had to take seriously—not someone who could easily be rolled because he was afraid of conflict or controversy. Reagan not only knew what he believed, but was willing to act on it even when that became difficult. The union bosses had to account for that in deciding how far to push on behalf of federal employees.

Reagan changed the culture, not just with words— although he was great with those—but with his deeds as well.

As it turned out, the firing of the PATCO strikers was also a political winner for Reagan. But he didn't do it for the politics. He did it because it was the right thing to do, and the political benefits of doing the right thing followed. Good leaders understand that.

I know a lot of my listeners and readers are not big fans of Karl Rove—and I have my issues with him too—but I still found a lot of value in a story he wrote in the *Wall Street Journal* about the first presidential campaign of George W. Bush.

You might recall that Bush initially asked Dick Cheney to lead the process of developing a short list of vice presidential contenders. Eventually, of course, Bush decided to ask Cheney himself to be his running mate. Rove wrote that he did not like the pick. It was nothing against Cheney personally, but Rove didn't think Cheney brought a lot of political benefits and potentially brought some real drawbacks to the ticket.

Before the pick was publicly announced, Rove explained, he went to Bush with a list of 10 problems Cheney would present, politically, as Bush's running mate. Bush read the list carefully, then looked at Rove and said (and I'm paraphrasing from memory here), You're right. These are problems. So solve them. My job is to make the right choice for the country. It's your job to make the politics work.[1]

That's what real leaders do. I'm not arguing that Bush approached every situation this way (and to be honest, neither did Reagan), but he understood this principle of leadership and applied it well in this situation. First you do what's right. Then you make the politics work.

I have often used an analogy to describe how effective leadership works. The acronym is W.A.R. and it works like this:

- Working on the right problems means changing the culture sometimes.
- Asking the right questions means identifying what needs changing.
- Removing barriers means making the sometimes tough calls to allow the culture to change.

These three steps are crucial to successful leadership, especially when a change in the organization's culture is necessary. That's what makes leadership like war.

Now how might our next president apply these principles? Clearly one difference between a private-sector CEO and the president is that a CEO doesn't have to deal with a co-equal legislative body. But he does have to make agreements. He has to make them with customers, employees, or shareholders... a good leader does more than just make decisions. He has to find out what's necessary to get people cooperating so that his decisions actually work.

The next president has to start exercising leadership by campaigning on a platform of solving the right problems. He (or she, Fiorina) has to make these issues central to the campaign, so that once he's won the election, everyone in Washington will understand that he was sent to Washington by the people to address those problems. Next, he has to go to the leaders of Congress in both parties and say, "Look, you know the priorities I campaigned on. These are the things I need to move on first. What do you need from me so I can get you on board with them?"

Then he should listen and carefully consider whether he can give the Congress what they say they need, or whether he can propose something different to get them on board. Sometimes you have to walk away from a deal if you're being asked for too much. Sometimes you have to settle for less than you want in order to avoid giving away too much.

When Bill Clinton was president and Newt Gingrich was Speaker of the House, the two of them dealt very effectively with each other. Clinton was a shrewd politician and he understood after the 1994 election that he couldn't ram through a left-wing agenda. So he worked with the Republican Congress on the things that were most important to him, and he let them have some things where he felt he could—including a cut in the capital gains tax that led to a huge spike in federal revenue and several years of budget surpluses.

Then, of course, Clinton took credit for it—even though capital gains tax cuts had traditionally been a very Republican idea. He didn't care. People were happy with the economy, and they loved the budget in surplus. Clinton was going to make sure everyone knew it happened on his watch. One of the reasons he was able to survive his own personal indiscretions and the impeachment drama is that we got good economic results from the combination of Clinton in the White House and the Republican Congress of that time period.

And that's because Clinton and Gingrich understood how to deal with each other.

If the 2016 election gives us a new Republican president while we maintain a Republican House and Senate—and I certainly hope that's the case—the new president might be tempted to think he will have an easy time of it with Congress. That would be a mistake. Members of Congress have their own priorities and agendas. Ask George W. Bush about his attempt to partially privatize Social Security, or his proposal to open up the ANWR for oil exploration. Just having Republican majorities on Capitol Hill did not bring him success. I don't know everything that was done to attempt to win those votes, but I know it didn't work.

A new president needs to approach Congress as potential partners in this process, but also has to have a sober view of what will be needed to bring Congress on board. The solutions we need to the problems we face would be seen as politically difficult according to the conventional wisdom of Washington D.C. Politicians hate taking political risks. But the right leader can get them on board, convince them to do the right thing first, and then get the politics right.

The right leader can also offer both the words and the actions that are necessary to change the culture of the federal government so these solutions can actually work. Without effective leadership from the right leader, none of this stands a chance.

# CHAPTER 8

## THE NEXT PRESIDENT

The New Chief Executive's Crucial
Top Priorities

If the United States is going to focus on solving the right problems, the leadership of the next president will be crucial. Nothing will do more to determine whether we can succeed with this effort.

The media often talk about what happens in a new president's first 100 days, as if there is something magical about that particular round number. It is absolutely true that a new leader's actions in the early going can either set the stage for success or send a message that nothing serious is going to happen. I talked in the Leadership chapter about actions I took right off the bat when I got my Burger King and Godfather's assignments. These actions established my leadership agenda and left people with a clear understanding of what was expected of them.

The president has to do that and more. His or her job is more difficult, because he is both a CEO who can call the shots within his administration and a political leader who must work with Congress and gain the support of the American people.

When the next president is inaugurated on January 20, 2017, here are some things he or she must do immediately:

### *Set the tone for the nation*

There's no question that a president who attacks the right problems set forth in this book is going to be seen as ideologically conservative. He should not pretend to be anything other than that. But a president can be strongly committed to his ideological principles and still be an inclusive leader for the entire country.

To understand this, we can start by looking to Barack Obama for what not to do. You don't cloak the White House in the colors of the rainbow flag after a Supreme Court ruling that legalizes gay marriage, because that tells those with sincere objections that you're only interested in spiking the football and rubbing it in their faces. You don't issue condemnations of police officers in situations where you're not even sure what the facts are, because that tells law enforcement across the country you're not really with them but instead interested in pandering to your left-wing base. You don't exploit horrific criminal acts by making them an excuse to push your gun-control agenda, because that tells the nation your agenda is more important to you than the victims and their families.

One of the reasons Obama is such a terrible president is that he doesn't think he's the leader of the entire nation. He thinks he's the leader of liberal Americans only, and he sees conservatives as the enemy.

Now some of you may want a conservative president to treat liberals as the enemy. If he doesn't, you'll complain that he's a squishy RINO. But it's a mistake to look at it that way. The president is the leader of the entire country, and he should be concerned about the well-being of his political opponents as well as that of his supporters.

I didn't say he should be accepting of his opponents' ideas if they're not good ones. He shouldn't. But he should work to implement policies that, once in place, benefit those who voted against him as well as for him. If the president is going to replace the tax code with a simpler code and lower rates, for example, he should do so in a way that benefits those areas that did not vote for him as well as those that did. If he's going to promote stronger business and job growth, he should be just as interested in seeing liberal Americans get better jobs as he is in seeing conservative Americans get them.

The president is the political leader of his party. But he's trusted with governing for the benefit of everyone. There is no contradiction between the two. When liberal ideas lose, liberals actually win because liberal ideas are bad ideas. They don't understand that, but it's true.

So when the new president talks to the nation about the priorities of his presidency, he should make it clear to Americans of all political stripes that his agenda is to make this a stronger nation for everyone—whether they voted for him or not.

He should say to people in urban areas: "I know many of you did not vote for me but I am going to pursue policies that I believe will make your cities safer and more livable."

He should say to feminists: "I know many of you did not vote for me but I want to pursue policies that make women safer and give women access to better opportunities in their careers."

He should say to union members: "I know many of you did not vote for me but I want to see you and your employers prosper and do well, and I will pursue policies that help make that happen."

And on and on he should go, and having said he wants to do these things, he should do them.

This doesn't mean that everyone who voted against him will automatically be won over or will instantly believe he means what he says or cares about them. Many will take a long time to get there. Some never will because they are so partisan that they're just not capable of it.

But by setting this tone, the president will let it be known that he does not consider it acceptable to view or talk about political opponents as enemies. They are not. They are people with ideas we disagree with, but still people whose lives we hope will go well. Obama has never set that tone. He has always made it clear that he considers people who don't agree with him to be beneath contempt. The new president must do exactly the opposite.

And this is more important than ever because he will be pursuing an agenda people on the left will already think is awful. The last thing the nation needs under those circumstances is to hear the president using triumphant rhetoric and talking about vanquished political opponents as if they are just trash to be taken out.

The objective here is not necessarily to gain the political support of those who have not supported him in the past, although it's possible it will at least gain some goodwill from them. More importantly, it's to let the nation know that the new president's priority is to govern, not to play politics. This will not only distinguish him from his predecessor, it will establish a different and much welcome expectation on the part of the nation.

### *Set the priorities*

Having set the proper tone, the new president must make it clear what his priorities are, and why. Both elements of this are crucial.

The reason I structured this book in the way I did was so you could understand not only the real problems I would emphasize, but why these are the leverage points that can do the most to enhance the overall health and prosperity of the nation.

The new president needs to tell the nation it's time to replace the tax code by emphasizing what a burden it is on them, but also by explaining how much it hinders job creation, capital formation and opportunities for growth. He needs to explain to them that the tax code is complicated mainly because that serves the interests of politicians who like to tinker and manipulate people's behavior. He needs to paint a picture for them of how much more simple and prosperous their lives would be if we had a new tax code.

The new president needs to tell the nation it's time to balance the budget by laying out the reality of our fiscal condition—the interest we're paying, the principle we have yet to touch, the forecasts for how this will mount in the coming years, and the likely tax burden on every American family if we keep amassing debt and have to finally face the music and pay it off. I don't think this will be a hard sell. The facts sell themselves. Politicians will wail that it can't be done but a strong leader who can make a good case can overcome that easily.

The new president needs to tell the nation about the energy resources we could be using and selling across the globe if only we would change our policies. He needs to explain that this is not only a massive opportunity for job creation but for a dramatic change in the economic dynamics of the entire world—in our favor. He needs to tell the people that the only thing stopping this from happening is bad government policies, and that it's crucial we change those policies quickly. The people will not have a difficult time understanding that.

The new president needs to tell the nation about the urgent imperative to secure the border and enforce our existing immigration laws. When the people understand that we have more than 11 million illegal aliens dwelling among us largely because we don't enforce existing laws, the people will understand it is not a radical idea to deal with the problem.[1] I realize that deporting 11 million illegals is aspirational, but it establishes the direction in which we need to move. The president also has to be clear and factual about the costs this problem is imposing on the nation—not only the economic cost but also the human cost from increased crime and the stress it's putting on law enforcement. Per the FBI, there were 67,642 murders in the U.S. from 2005 through 2008, and 115,717 from 2003 through 2009.[2] Per the GAO, criminal aliens committed 25,064 of them. That means they committed 22% to 37% of all murders in the U.S., while being only 3.52% to 8.25% of the population. Conclusion: criminal and illegal aliens commit murder at much higher rates than all inhabitants of the U.S. – at least 3 to 10 times higher."[3]

The new president needs to tell the nation about the crushing impact of the regulatory state on businesses and individuals, and explain the need to get rid of regulations wherever they cannot be justified both by economics and by common sense. He needs to acknowledge that some regulations are useful for public health and safety, but that far too many serve no purpose other than to allow some politician or bureaucrat to advance a pet agenda. When the people understand the resources that are sucked up by regulatory compliance—resources that could be used to create jobs and bring about greater private-sector prosperity—they will support this imperative.

The new president needs to tell the nation that Social Security is not just fine—as Democrats forever insist it is—and that Americans have been sold a bill of goods with the notion that a benefit is guaranteed simply because the government says they're going to get it. He needs to simply but clearly present the numbers, including the truth about how Congress routinely raids the so-called Social Security Trust Fund (which in reality doesn't exist) so they can paper over the real size of the budget deficit.[4] And he needs to tell them what has worked better in other countries like Canada and Chile, thus disabusing them of the notion that trusting the government is safe but trusting private markets is some sort of wild and irresponsible scheme. This will be a difficult political challenge because the new president will be attacked by the senior lobby and by entrenched interests who are determined to never let Social Security be changed. But if he calmly answers all the hysteria with facts and steadfastly points the way forward, the people will get behind him.

The president needs to tell the nation that Medicare and Medicaid, like Social Security, represent a mounting future obligation that will bankrupt the nation if we let it. The numbers are daunting. We're talking about more than $100 trillion in looming obligations.[5] The president should present this information not in an alarmist way but simply to help the people understand why we cannot sustain the promises that have been made. And he should tell them that there are perfectly good alternatives—like federal support for premiums to private insurers—that can meet people's needs while allowing the federal government to keep its financial obligation manageable. The president also needs to make it clear that ObamaCare has made this problem much worse, and that he will be signing a repeal of ObamaCare as soon as Congress puts it on his desk.

The president needs to confront the American people with the urgency of rebuilding our military, explaining the strategic, human and geopolitical price we've already paid—in Iran, Libya, Syria, Ukraine, Iraq and so many other places—because of both our refusal and our inability to confront the bad actors across the globe. He should make it clear that this in no way means we intend armed conflict in every one of these situations—or for that matter, in any of them necessarily. But rather, that America's foes have historically backed down from making trouble when they knew we had both the will and the capacity to take them on. He should understand that Americans have become weary of war after the long struggles in Iraq and Afghanistan, but should also make clear that war is often prevented when America avoids falling into weakness in the first place.

And finally, the president should make clear that his administration will return to a respect for this nation's laws and for its Constitution. Barack Obama has run roughshod over both. He has refused to enforce laws he doesn't like, or that are politically inconvenient to him, and he has simply helped himself to executive power that the Constitution does not grant him. Conservatives will be tempted to hope a new Republican president fights fire with fire and does the exact same thing. But this would be a mistake. Solving the right problems as laid out in this book will be difficult enough. It would be impossible to do without the consent of the governed—the very thing that would prompt Congress to get on board and pave the way for a legal and constitutional pursuit of the right solutions to the right problems.

### *Educate the people*

I do not want another president who tries to govern by giving speeches. We've seen all too well where that gets us. But the problem with Obama is that he thought all he had to do was make a speech and talk about the way things should be, and suddenly it would be that way. He wasn't willing to do the hard work of governing, nor did he have the skills to do so. The next president has to both work hard to implement these policies and to sell them to the American people.

A single address to the nation will not do it. That's just the start. The president needs to embark on an aggressive effort to educate the nation about the policies he's proposing, and to counter the criticisms that will inevitably come from the left. He needs to give interviews, make public appearances and use social media to its full advantage. He even needs to be willing to appear on liberal shows and deal with liberal interviewers—although he needs to be careful not to think it's his job to please these people. That's a fool's game and it never works for any Republican. You can't win them over but you can engage them and demonstrate that the facts are on your side, and that you're not afraid of the onslaught.

I really don't want to see a lot of these staged events where the president's political people pack the arena with handpicked supporters—especially those silly things where you see the consultant-selected group sitting behind him. There is no need for that. I don't want a president who embarks on a perpetual campaign. Two of our last three presidents have done that. But the president has to be willing to engage the people and do everything in his power to ensure they understand his proposals—what they will do and why they are necessary.

### Internal imperatives

The president is an executive leader in charge of a very large and complex organization. He cannot lead it effectively if he doesn't choose the right people to serve as his deputies, and if he doesn't make it clear to each of them what he expects of them.

The president should start by setting a personal policy that cabinet selections will not be for the purpose of rewarding supporters or pleasing constituencies. Everyone knows that Barack Obama picked Hillary Clinton to be Secretary of State in order to placate her supporters, and because he apparently believes the saying, "Keep your friends close and your enemies closer."

But that is no way to run an organization that you expect to produce results. The new president needs to select cabinet secretaries who have particular competencies, not only in management but also in the particular department they're being asked to run. Some government experience is probably helpful because there are a lot of political machinations to deal with, but it is more important that the Treasury Secretary understands finance, and that the Commerce Secretary understands business, and that the Defense Secretary understands the military and national security issues. And so on.

And it is equally important that each cabinet secretary is fully committed to the president's goals. He needs to sit down personally with each person he's considering and do what is necessary to find that out.

Here's a technique I often used when I was hiring managers to work under me. I would lay out a goal I had, and then ask them, "How would you achieve this?" Then I would just sit back and let them talk. How they responded spoke volumes. You could easily tell if the person didn't really believe in the goal and was just trying to tell me what he thought I wanted to hear. You could tell if he maybe agreed with the goal but had no idea what to do with it. However the new president wants to achieve this, he absolutely must make sure that his cabinet secretaries are on board.

Not only that, he has to make sure they are prepared to exercise strong leadership over the federal bureaucracy, because the greatest resistance to change will probably come from there. Entrenched federal employees will use everything from civil service protection to their own informal networks of influence to thwart the president's agenda. Often, cabinet secretaries have been completely helpless against this passive/aggressive resistance from their underlings. The president needs to hire strong executive leaders who know what to do and are willing to do it.

I also think it would be worth the president's time to meet directly with the employees of some of these departments, laying out his expectations to them directly, and making it clear that their direct reports will be holding to these standards. This sends a message that the president is serious about the goals and that he is willing to invest his personal time in making sure the employees are behind them as well.

That doesn't eliminate all possibility of bureaucratic resistance, but it does raise the stakes in the game when the president has personally come to tell you what his expectations are. Are you sure you want to defy him after he's taking things to that extent?

Believe me, it matters in executive leadership. All of these steps do.

# CHAPTER 9

## THE VOICE OF THE PEOPLE

### Americans Don't View Problems Anything Like Their Political Leaders Do

I talk to regular Americans every day. And often at night. I talk to them on the phone, over the radio and in person during college campus appearances, and during keynote addresses I am asked to make on a regular basis. And I don't just talk to them. I listen to them, too.

One thing I can tell you from having this much contact with people all over the country is that there is a huge gap between the way normal people think and the way political people think. To call it a gap is putting it mildly. It's more like the Grand Canyon, or maybe the Pacific Ocean.

At the heart of it is this: Normal people don't understand why leaders can't solve problems. That's because normal people solve problems in their own lives with regularity. If their spending is outpacing their income, they make adjustments. If they're paying too much for car insurance, they switch insurers. If their grass is too long, they cut it. If their kitchen is filthy, they clean it.

And most of them work for employers who do the same thing. If costs are out of control, things are cut. If a major customer is lost, a new one is pursued. If an idea isn't working, it's discarded. If an employee isn't cutting it, the employee is fired.

Normal people don't just sit around and let problems persist indefinitely. They also don't deny the reality of problems that are plain as day to anyone paying attention. I realize there are some individuals who act like this, and you can usually spot those people. They struggle in their lives. They are chronically unemployed or underemployed. They have low self-esteem. They are the people that other people are always trying to help—usually with frustrating results because it's very difficult to get a person to change when the person doesn't want to. In fact, I'd say it's impossible.

So you recognize those people because they stick out like sore thumbs. But you also recognize that well-adjusted people who know how to function in society don't act like this. They solve problems, address issues and make adjustments where necessary so they can live well and do well. They don't deny reality. They don't blame others. And they don't shrink from responsibility. In fact, really effective people like responsibility because when you're responsible for what happens, you're empowered to make a difference.

And this is what most of the people with whom I talk every day are like. They solve problems in their own lives, and they can't make any sense of why political leaders cannot, or will not, solve the nation's problems.

That's because it makes no sense.

And as you might expect, regular people talk about things that the political class and their media mouthpieces don't. One example is the rise in taxes coupled with the fall in median incomes. The political class thinks concern about taxes is just a right-wing talking point. Normal people feel this, and they feel it profoundly in their lives.

For the political class, discussions about taxation are framed in one of two ways. Either they take the form of ideological debates, in which conservatives and liberals debate theory and talking points, or they come in the context of whether the government is getting enough money from the taxpayers. For the people I hear from every day, a discussion of taxes concerns whether they will have enough left to pay their bills, and maybe save a little once they've paid them all to the government. When politicians say that raising taxes is the "responsible thing to do" because that way all their spending is "fully funded," what they tend to leave out is that they are confiscating money from the people who earned it, and as a result of that confiscation those people will now find it much more difficult to fully fund their lives.

It takes a person steeped in the delusion of the political class not to understand or care about this side of the equation, or to think it makes no impact on the nation's vitality as a whole.

Another thing people talk to me about on a regular basis is the lack of economic growth we've seen over the course of the past decade or so. The media would have you believe that the economy is "bouncing back" or whatever because we occasionally see annual growth slightly above 2 percent—and on a very rare occasion during the Obama administration it's exceeded 3 or even 4 percent for a calendar quarter.[1]

People know better. They don't believe the administration's excuses for two straight first-quarter declines in GDP. When it happened in the first quarter of 2014, the administration tried to blame the unusually harsh winter. When it happened again in the first quarter of 2015 (following a more normal winter), the administration just wanted to change the subject.

Do you think the average person can't tell when someone is just trying to come up with excuses?

The same is true on the employment front. The media would also have you believe that we're creating a lot of jobs because sometimes we hear about 200,000 new jobs or more in a given month.

But real people notice that this spin doesn't square with their real-life experience. For one thing, people who are willing to give it a little thought can run the numbers. In a nation consisting of more than 320 million people and growing every day, it's little more than a blip to add 200,000 jobs in a month when unemployment claims are nearly 300,000 a week. Think about it like this: You've got 50 states, and in every state you've got how many individual communities, big and small? Take those 200,000 jobs and start dividing them up among all those individual communities, and then divide them up among all the neighborhoods. Pretty soon you realize that you need a lot more job creation than that to really make a significant impact on people's lives.

Americans are not stupid. They can figure this out. And they feel it in their own lives, too. They know that their employers are still being careful, and that they're not confident that economic growth is either robust enough or sustained enough to make major new additions to their payrolls.

On our show we don't just parrot the unemployment figures that come from the Department of Labor. We also explain what they mean, and that includes the fact that the U-3 unemployment rate doesn't include people who have dropped out of the workforce.[2] We tell them that actual labor force participation is as low as it's been at any point since the Carter administration.

People understand what this means. It's easy to make the unemployment rate look good if you don't count people who aren't even trying. And everyone knows people like that. Those in the political class probably don't because they don't operate in the real world. But normal people do.

You rarely hear politicians talk about labor force participation, and that's for a variety of reasons. Some of them don't know how to turn it into a talking point. I suspect a lot of them don't really understand what it means. Maybe some are afraid that if they talk about people giving up, they'll be accused of "blaming the victim." But normal people understand exactly what it means. They see folks so frustrated by the state of the economy that they figure there's little point in even trying.

Another thing people talk to me about is their frustration over the refusal of politicians to make decisions on matters like the Keystone XL pipeline. This is a beautiful example of the fantasy world in which politicians operate.

The Obama administration has been dragging its feet on approval of the pipeline for nearly seven years. That is not because it's a difficult decision. It's a very easy decision. Approve the pipeline, promote the creation of new jobs, get the oil to market, reduce the amount of oil being shipped by truck and train. That's about as easy as a decision can be. The problem is that it's a difficult political calculation. Environmental groups oppose it because they hate the oil industry, and they'll be enraged if the project is approved.

But you can't very well forbid it without a reason, and there is simply no reason the project should not be built.

So what does the Obama administration do? They sit on it. They claim it is still "under review" even though everyone knows they just don't want to make a decision.

The people I hear from can't imagine operating that way in their own lives. Imagine that your boss asked you to study a matter and bring him a recommendation so he could make a decision. How long do you think you could get away with not giving him the recommendation, telling him instead that you're "still reviewing" it? You know perfectly well what would happen.

Get me that report by the end of the day or you're out of here!

Only in government can people refuse to do their job for seven years and pay no price for it. But people in the real world notice it, and they aren't fooled by the explanations of the political class. They completely understand what's going on.

Another example is Obama's efforts to shut down the coal industry with regulations that make it virtually impossible for coal to operate legally. That's because real people understand what this means. Coal is one of America's most plentiful sources of energy, with a 500-year supply that God did not give us because He wanted us to let it sit there without being used.[3] Making it impossible to mine and produce coal as an energy source creates energy scarcity, and real people are not fooled when Obama says we can simply rely more on wind and solar. It would be great if we could, but everyone knows these energy sources are not yet reliable enough to power us as coal does.[4]

To a normal person, this simply makes no sense. You don't go to war against a plentiful and necessary energy source just because you have an ideological problem with it. And you don't tell people to rely on something that's fundamentally unreliable in its place.

What I hear on college campuses is no different. In fact, when I talk to young people I get a very different sense of their priorities than the impression you get from the political class and their media mouthpieces.

For one thing, college students hardly ever bring up social issues. The political class thinks that all it has to do to keep college-age people happy is talk up gay marriage and make sure they have all the access they want to contraceptives and abortion. They think young people are nothing more than party animals who want to get drunk and have sex all the time with no consequences. The real young people who come to see me are concerned about their economic futures. They care about their job prospects. They're concerned about the debt they'll take out of college and about their prospects for earning enough money to ever pay it off.

Now let's be honest: Most of them would probably be supportive if Democrats simply decided—as many would like to do—to simply forgive their student loans. Few groups of people will look a gift horse in the mouth. But they're not coming up to me and demanding that. What they want is a chance to make it in the real world, and they're starting to wonder if what they're getting at state universities is really going to equip them to compete for the best jobs and to do well in them.

They're asking the right questions. The political class responds to this by shoveling more money in the direction of colleges and universities, and by proposing—as Hillary Clinton did on the day this chapter was written—hundreds of billions of federal dollars to make college either free or very cheap.

But young people see that for the scam it is. More funding for the college doesn't mean it does a better job of preparing you for your career. And making it free for you doesn't increase its value. In fact, anyone who understands basic economics knows that when you make something free you really reduce its value—because now anyone can get it, and it means nothing that you have it.

Young people want to know one thing: How do they make it? What decisions should they make? What priorities should they set? What should they know? This is what's important to them. And they're starting to understand that easy money—in the form of student loans from the government—is not the blessing they thought it was. These are hard lessons, but they're figuring things out.

Oh, by the way, college students hate ObamaCare. One of the most absurd suppositions of the political class was that young people would be thrilled because ObamaCare would allow them to stay on their parents' insurance until they are 26. They don't see that as anything to celebrate! They want to be able to see themselves as independent and taking care of their own needs by the time they're 26. The prospect of relying on their parents at 26 is not something they want to shoot for. It's something they want to avoid.

They do, however, ask whether Social Security will be there for them when they retire. But they don't have much hope that it will, which I'd say is a positive insofar as it's encouraging them to do their own saving for retirement. It's not hard for them to see that the outdated model of Social Security can't be sustained over the long term unless it's radically changed. And again, they understand that the refusal of politicians to make these changes comes from fear of reprisals, not from a sober understanding of the problem and how to solve it.

I am not suggesting that leaders should make their decisions by polling the public and just doing what the greatest number of people want. That's not leadership. That's pandering, and we've already got enough of that. But what I am suggesting is that leaders should hear the people and understand their priorities.

You may believe you've got a better solution to the problem of unemployment, but don't sit there talking about global warming while people want you to do something about jobs.

You may believe and think your ideas on economic growth are better than what the opinion polls suggest people want, but don't tell us we're doing just great when we can barely get above 2 percent growth most of the time.

You may think you've got an energy strategy that beats what other people have. That's fine. But don't go to war against coal and tell people to rely on things that everyone knows are not reliable. That's just nonsense.

And you might not like the pipeline proposal. But don't tell us you've been "reviewing it" for seven years when everyone knows you're just afraid to make a decision.

This is the fundamental chasm that exists in America. The left/right divide is real, and it matters, but more important is the divide between political people and non-political people. This is one of the things I found out when I ran for president. I had an existing staff of people who had worked for me at T.H.E. New Voice, and I figured it made sense to coordinate the efforts of those folks with those of my political team. So as I brought on political advisors, I set about trying to get the two groups functioning as one seamless unit.

That was much more difficult than I expected it to be, because people in the political world don't think like people in the world where you and I operate. They can say the same words but mean totally different things. They can look at a set of facts and understand them in a totally different way. Their priorities are different. Their presumptions are different. Their definitions of success and failure are totally different.

My nonpolitical staff had a very difficult time with that, and honestly, so did I. Even though I was the candidate, my thinking was decidedly in the camp of the "normal" people. Even so, I tried as the leader to get both groups to work well together. People learn in the cultures where they operate. Some of the political people were excellent at what they did. It's just that the nature of what they did was difficult to make work with the methods of those who are not from that world—and that's most of us.

So when you hear normal people speaking one language and expressing certain priorities, while political people speak an entirely different language and express completely different priorities, welcome to my world. This is what I see and hear every single day.

I am convinced that if all 435 congressional districts in this country were to elect representatives who had never been in politics before—regardless of party—problems would be solved. Even those of different ideological bents would recognize the imperative of working through their disagreements to get to solutions. After all, this is what normal people do in their day-to-day lives, if only because they have no choice.

You can't simply leave problems unsolved. That's unacceptable and someone will hold you accountable if you do. Only in the political world can you do that, and maybe that's why a certain class of people is attracted to politics.

Unfortunately, these are the very people who absolutely will never work on the right problems and will never choose the right solutions. They should start listening to the voice of the people—like I do every day.

# CHAPTER 10

## WHY I STILL BELIEVE IN THE AMERICAN DREAM

### The Vital Assets That Position Us to Once Again Lead the World

I've spent the first nine chapters of this book talking about how we can identify the right problems to work on in this country, and how we can solve them. I've talked about what leaders should do to make this happen, and I've also talked about why people who pose as leaders don't really want to make it happen.

What I haven't talked about, until now, is why this nation is so worth saving from the calamities that await if we don't solve these problems.

Now your initial reaction to that statement might be, "It's obvious why America is worth saving. We don't need to be told that."

But I don't think we should take for granted that everyone understands this. Generally speaking, I think most Americans agree that this is a great and powerful nation, and that it's a force for good in the world. I think we all agree that the freedoms guaranteed in our Constitution have helped to make and keep this a very special place.

But do we really understand the value and the power of the assets that still reside in this country?

There is a video that's been floating around on social media for some time now from the TV show The Newsroom. In the clip, Jeff Daniels is in character as Will McAvoy, a big-time news anchor who certainly appears to me to be a liberal. (So I guess he fits in.) If you search for this clip on social media you'll see that it's almost always liberals who share it.

McAvoy is participating in a panel discussion and a young woman asks the panelists what makes America the greatest nation on Earth. The first two panelists give fairly punchless, cliché-type answers. When McAvoy's turn comes up, he shocks everyone by declaring that America is not the greatest nation on Earth, and proceeds to cite a litany of statistics to prove his point. (How he has all these statistics memorized is beyond me, but I guess that's why we're supposed to think he's so smart.)

Ultimately he becomes quite insulting toward the young woman who asked the question, and by the end everyone is shooting video of his anti-American rant. This is the clip liberals love to share on social media, and it's clear to me that this is how many of them view the country.

Well. They're wrong. America remains great in spite of the horrible leaders we presently have. And America's assets are strong and worth saving.

I am really not interested in getting into a battle of statistical studies with a fictional TV character to prove that I'm right and he's wrong. If America is falling behind in some areas, it's no wonder, since our leaders have refused for so long to solve our problems. But this nation absolutely has exceptional strengths that will put us in position to bounce back and be a world leader once again—if only we will start making better decisions in the areas discussed in this book.

I want to tell you about some of them:

### Consumer Purchasing Power

Let's start with consumer purchasing power, which is really a product of our standard of living. This represents 60 percent of the entire calculation of the nation's GDP,[1] so we're talking about more than $10 trillion a year in spending.[2] Liberals sometimes talk about America's standard of living as if it represents some sort of moral crime. The reason we live so well is because Americans earn a lot of money and have a lot to spend. That's why middle-class people have flat-screen televisions, spa-sized bathrooms and satellite dishes. It's not because we're decadent and selfish. It's because people have the money to spend and businesses are smart enough to make the products they want to buy.

This is a very good thing. A nation with that kind of purchasing power can sustain a robust private-sector-led economy over a long period of time. If what we need to pay off the national debt is an economy that grows at a rapid pace over a long period of time (and it is), a workforce that's capable of producing on that level is an absolute necessity. Not every country has that kind of capacity. We do. Americans work, they earn, they spend, and they generate wealth.

And while the Obama administration is trying very hard to re-order our economy to focus on redistribution of wealth rather than the creation of wealth, that is still not the way most Americans think or behave. The culture of this nation still favors self-reliance through hard work and productivity. There is no other nation on Earth where that is as true as it is here, and if released from the shackles currently imposed by ridiculous government, this economy can and will produce at that level again.

## Productive Capacity

There's another side to the equation we introduced by talking about consumer purchasing power, and that's the productive capacity of the private sector. America's business community has tremendous physical infrastructure, plenty of capital and access to natural resources. It also has experienced people who came up in a business-focused culture and understand how to invest, produce, sell and expand.

The business sector is unduly burdened at the moment by the corporate tax as well as by taxes on dividends and capital gains, and it doesn't help that government imposes wage minimums and tends to tip the scales in favor of unions whenever it can. And yet America's business community is strong and productive, serving the demands of consumers with purchasing power and a very clear idea of what they want to buy.

The thought of what American business could do without all the obstacles government throws up is pretty exciting to me. And it's all the more true when you realize the potential of the American energy sector without the federal government constantly blocking access to oil, natural gas and coal resources. Unleash those resources and just imagine what American industry could do with them.

### *Abundant Food*

Another strong asset America enjoys is one whose importance you might overlook, but you shouldn't. It's abundant food. A lot of countries struggle just to make sure their citizens have access to basic food necessities. Sometimes that's a product of their geography—too hot, too dry or too rocky for agriculture to flourish. Sometimes it's a product of political corruption. We've all heard stories of American food donations showing up in poor African nations, only to disappear before they ever reach the people who need the food because the corrupt governments, or anti-government rebels, got their hands on the shipments first.

Whatever the reasons, plentiful access to food is far from a given in many nations on Earth. Because food is so plentiful here, it is relatively inexpensive and almost everyone can afford to purchase all they need without assistance beyond their own income. And for those who do need help, society can provide the help in a relatively affordable manner.

Now I realize this has been tipping in the wrong direction in recent years. Obama's policies now see more than 46 million Americans on food stamps, and that is way too many.[3] But it's not because we don't have enough food. It's because too many people earn too little money, and they have too little of their income left after purchasing their food for other necessities of life. Yet even during a time when we find ourselves assisting way too many people with access to food, we still don't struggle to have enough.

This is not to say government isn't capable of messing this up. Notorious policies of paying farmers not to grow crops, or of subsidizing corn for the production of ethanol instead of food, are classic cases of price manipulation that serve the agendas of politicians and private interests instead of markets as whole.

But America's capacity to produce enough food on a sustained basis, given our plentiful farming technology, abundant livestock and fertile agricultural land, is going to exist no matter what the government does. The reason this is so crucial to sustained economic growth is simple: If you need to use up all your resources to meet basic needs, you have nothing left to invest in higher-value pursuits. America does not suffer from that problem, and that gives us a leg up over much of the world.

### Shelter

The same is true of shelter. If you can remember the 1980s, you'll recall that President Reagan was criticized by liberals for "cutting the housing budget,"[4] and they said that this had resulted in widespread homelessness. That was nonsense then, and it's nonsense today.

America has abundant housing resources, much of it sitting vacant. People find themselves homeless because they don't have a job, can't earn enough income, or choose not to take the responsibility, and that results from any number of factors. But there's a big difference between certain people failing to secure a necessity and there not being enough of the necessity to go around.

Not only do we have plenty of housing, but when we see a boom housing market, we have plenty of housing development companies with the capacity to crank out new affordable housing in record time.

Even the collapse of the mortgage market in 2008 wasn't because we had too little housing. It was because too much money was invested in housing by people who overestimated its potential as an investment. If you've invested in something and there's very little of it, you stand to do pretty well. But when there's enough or more than enough, you're going to have a hard time making your money back, since buyers have lots of other options besides what you're offering.

In fact, we can point to government forays into the construction of housing as making the situation worse, not better. Anyone who's heard about the notorious Cabrini Green tenement complex in Chicago knows this.[5] The federal government subsidized this nightmare of an apartment building on the theory that there wasn't enough affordable housing available, so they had to get into the business and undercut everyone else's rents. How did that go? About how you'd expect. The building became a magnet for crime and drugs and proved to be a destination that people in Chicago knew they should avoid at all costs.

That's what happens when you make housing too cheap. You reduce the accountability or on the part of those who live there, and the results are never pretty when that happens. Instead of government trying to make housing affordable, perhaps government should create a path to ownership. Only then would the residents have a sense of skin in the game.

### Clothing and Shoes

The same is true with things like clothing and shoes. Americans stand there in the morning trying to decide what to wear because they have so many options. They don't just have a pair of shoes. They have a closet full of them. I know this doesn't apply to everyone, but this is a very common experience for many people in this country—and I'm sure that's true for many who are reading this book. Many Americans don't realize how atypical this experience is throughout much of the world, where people are just happy to have anything to put on, let alone an abundance of options.

And this all comes back to consumer purchasing power and the business community's capacity to produce—both of which feed each other. When government gets out of the way and lets them both happen unimpeded, folks have plenty of what they want and the economy is growing.

Now this is usually where liberals say that all this wealth is exactly why people should be paying more in taxes. It's not right, liberals say, that people have so much but the government doesn't have enough. Of course they've got that backwards. Lower tax rates allow all this activity to flourish, producing wealth and providing government enough resources to do its job from a larger tax base. Plus, since so many people have enough, there is less stress on government to step in and meet people's needs.

If liberals really wanted government to be effective, they would cheer private-sector wealth, because private sector wealth expands the tax base that finances government while reducing the demands on government. The only reason they have the attitude they do toward wealth is that they want all power concentrated in government, including the power to decide who can have how much money and things.

## *Highway Infrastructure*

Here is another huge asset the United States has, and for this I am going to credit the federal government for making it happen: our highway system. It was the vision and leadership of President Dwight D. Eisenhower in the 1950s that gave us the highway system we have today, along with the willing support of the Congress we had at that time. In the aftermath of World War II, much federal spending was diverted from the erstwhile war effort to the building of the roads and bridges that would be necessary to sustain a growing economy.

Most Americans are not old enough to remember what it was like before we had the highways, but those who do will recall that the building of the highways was as much about the nation's military readiness as about its private economy. To understand this, try to imagine what it would be like to drive from New York to California on secondary roads. Not much fun, right? Now try to imagine that you're commanding the nation's military and you need to move munitions across the country to defend our shores against a prospective attack. That's what the military had to do in World War II, when Eisenhower served as Supreme Allied Commander. When he became president, he was determined to see that America's infrastructure could support both its business activity and its military readiness.

Now maybe some of you are not happy that I'm naming an asset that we enjoy because of the federal government.

Maybe some of you think I sound like Barack Obama, who is constantly yelping about the need to spend more money on roads and bridges. Let me explain why you should not be troubled.

For one thing, when Obama demands money for infrastructure, it's nothing more than an excuse to increase the federal budget baseline and ultimately to raise taxes. Democrats always want to spend more money, and they'll talk up the idea by emphasizing things people are generally willing to support. Once they've confiscated your money, of course, they'll spend it on whatever they want.

When I laud the federal government's infrastructure spending in the '50s, I'm lauding an approach that rightly focused on one of the things that is truly a proper role for government. I am not anti-government. I am anti-big government, and I am against government trying to do things that people can and should do for themselves. I'm also against government trying to do so many things that it becomes unwieldy, unmanageable and ineffective. (See: Right now.) But I want an effective government to have the resources to do what is needed of it, and that absolutely includes building and maintaining highways. This has been good for the country. If Obama wants more money for highways, he should stop pouring so much money into ObamaCare. People can buy their own health care. They can't build their own highways.

## *Domestic Energy Resources*

Another enormous asset—referenced above and as-yet mostly untapped—is our domestic energy resources. We have the resources to lead the world in energy development, although we don't at the moment because Congress has put together a series of regulations that prevent this from happening. That includes restrictions against drilling leases on federally owned lands and on lands declared off-limits for the purpose of environmental protection. It also includes restrictions on the construction of new refineries. And of course, America has maintained a ban on oil exports since the oil crisis of the 1970s. We discussed that in one of the previous chapters, so I don't need to go into exhaustive detail about it here. But energy is a classic example of a powerful asset we're just not taking advantage of.

I want to touch on two more assets that are less tangible but in my mind just as important.

## *Our Constitution*

The first is our Constitution. Not that it's much valued by the political class, but the Constitution is an absolutely brilliant blueprint for a government that is limited by definition and that right from the start concedes far more power to the people than it keeps for itself.

Of course, the Constitution is just a document. It can't enforce itself. And if you get a president who flouts it, a

Supreme Court that ignores it, and a Congress that's afraid to assert it, then you can't blame the document itself for losing its effectiveness. But what can restore the Constitution to its rightful place in our nation's journey is if the people demand leaders that respect and follow it. It hasn't appeared that we've been going in that direction during the Obama years, as more people seem interested in free stuff than freedom. But I still believe the American people will choose the right priorities when they have all the information, and if they are reminded of the value of the system of government the Founders gave us, they will resume demanding respect for the Constitution.

This is not about who wins ideological battles. It's about ensuring that a government designed to serve the people does not drift into tyranny. That above all is what the Founders designed the Constitution to do. And it would still be effective if we demanded our leaders operate according to its limits and constraints.

No other country has a Constitution like ours, and we need to not only preserve it but return it to pre-eminence in our public life.

### *Our Faith*

And the last asset I want to mention is our faith tradition. The sad fact is that the rest of the world is generally a much more secular place than America. I realize that in today's culture it is by no means universal that we still celebrate this tradition. But it's part of what's made us strong and unique throughout our history. People argue about whether the Founders intended this to be a Christian nation or a Judeo-Christian nation. Some try to tell you they were all atheists.

My own belief is that you take a group of men like that and put them all into one box. I'm sure there were strong Christian believers among the Founders, as well as others who were ambivalent or not believers at all. But what you can't deny is that the Judeo-Christian ethic is all over our founding documents—and that reflects the faith tradition that was prominent in the colonies at the time, and has remained prominent throughout our storied history.

Our faith tradition has made families strong. It has given rise to churches who have served as vital institutions. It's generated billions to support hospitals, shelters, food pantries and many other worthy organizations. It's also served to restrain some of our worst instincts as people. Why do you think America has served as a beacon of hope for the world, and as a defender of free people? Why do you think we are so often the first to respond when people around the world are in need?

Don't tell me our faith tradition isn't a major driver behind these virtues. Anyone can see that it is.

This is a very wonderful nation. We've got a heroic history, an unmatched track record and much potential for a great future. We are truly exceptional, and not in the very conditional way President Obama says it. ("I believe in American exceptionalism, just as I'm sure the Brits believe in British exceptionalism and the Greeks believe in Greek exceptionalism."[6]) No. There is no nation on Earth that can match our assets, our values, our traditions and our achievements.

Not. A. Single. One. Obama doesn't want to admit that, but it's the truth.

That's why I still believe in the American Dream, and I think it's important that Americans understand why it's so important to focus on the right problems and apply the right solutions. This nation is worth saving for so many reasons.

And I do mean saving. We are strong, but no nation's survival is guaranteed if it persists in fiscal delusion and political malfeasance. If we don't address the problems we've discussed here, we can't be so arrogant as to say, "It doesn't matter. We're America. Nothing can take us down."

I would certainly agree that no external foe can ever take us down. But no nation can rise above its own refusal to face the facts and deal with them. This book lays out a game plan for attacking our problems with high-leverage solutions that will leave us stronger, more prosperous and better positioned to take advantage of the greatest assets any nation ever had.

No matter who we elect in 2016, I invite them to take it and make it their own. The opportunity to live in a renewed and restored America will serve as more than enough credit for me.

THE END . . . Now let's begin!

# ACKNOWLEDGMENTS

Acknowledgements and Thanks!

Dan Calabrese for his ideas and help with the
manuscript

Lisa Reichert for her meticulous review and
coordination of the book

Clark Barrow for his assistance with identifying
attribution sources

Melanie Cain Gallo, Angie Calabrese, Jerry
Strober, Deborah Strober

Listeners to my Radio Show who helped inspire
me to write this book

# AFTERWORD

After reading this book you will be better **informed** about what we need to do to get this great nation back on the right track. We are not on the right track with a sluggish economy, a smaller military, out of control national debt, and a foggy ineffective foreign policy. Solving the right problems will get us going.

But we all have to be **involved!** The politicians don't do the right things unless we apply the heat for them to see the light. Just look at how much has not been solved in the past two decades. We have not been applying enough heat often enough. Now you have a tool to do that with, *The Right Problems.*

Everybody can do something to be involved! Even if it's making sure you vote, and encouraging others to vote the right way. The right information that's credible and logical is a powerful weapon against those who are clueless, or against those that want more government, more taxes on the people, and more people dependent on a government "program."

If you read this book you want less government, less taxes on the people, and less people dependent on a government "program."

When we are properly **informed** and **involved** we will find those nuggets of reason to be **inspired** to reject the negative and defeatist rhetoric that this nation is beyond the tipping point toward socialism.

We are not beyond the tipping point!

At least not for me, because I have four nuggets of inspiration to continue to believe we must begin to fix the mess we are in, despite the denial by too many people that we are not in a national directional mess.

My nuggets of inspiration are my four grandchildren.

Who are yours?

Whoever they are, let's start working on "The Right Problems."

# END NOTES

**Chapter One**

[1] Boriss, Steve. 2008. "AP's new 'accountability journalism' is a sham". http://pjmedia.com/blog/aps-new-accountability-journalism-is-a-sham/

[2] Roff, Peter. 2013. "Who's checking the fact checkers?" *US News & World Report.* http://www.usnews.com/opinion/blogs/peter-roff/2013/05/28/study-finds-fact-checkers-biased-against-republicans

**Chapter Two**

[1] USDebtclock.org 2015. http://usdebtclock.org/

[2] Campbell, Colin. 2015. "Hillary Clinton called for 'toppling' the 1%." *Business Insider.* http://www.businessinsider.com/report-hillary-clinton-called-for-toppling-the-1-2015-4

## Chapter Three

[1] Congressional Budget Office. 2015. "The Budget and Economic Outlook: 2015-2025." Congressional Budget Office. http://www.cbo.gov/sites/default/files/cbofiles/attachments/49892-Outlook2015.pdf

[2] Ibid.

[3] Ibid.

[4] Penner, Rudolph. 2013. "Are low interest rates masking the deficit?" *The Christian Science Monitor.* http://www.csmoitor.com/Business/Tax-VOX/2013/0710/Are-low-interest-rates-masking-the-deficit

[5] $18,000,000,000,000 divided by 90 years = $200,000,000,000

[6] The White House. 2015. "Historical Tables." Office of Management and Budget. https://www.whitehouse.gov/omb/budget/Historicals

[7] de Rugy, Veronica. 2012. "How many workers support one social security retiree?" George Mason University Mercatus Center. http://mercatus.org/publication/how-many-workers-support-one-social-security-retiree

[8] U.S. Census Bureau. 2015. "Births, deaths, marriages & divorces: Life expectancy." U.S. Census Bureau. http://www.census.gov/compendia/statab/cats/births_deaths_marriages_divorces/life_expectancy.html

[9] Social Security Administration. 2015. "Social security is important to young people." Social Security Press Office. http://www.ssa.gov/newes/press/factsheets/young.htm

[10] John, David C. 2004. "Misleading the public: How the social security trust fund really works." The Heritage Foundation. http://www.heritage.org/research/reports/2004/09/misleading-the-public-how-the-social-security-trust-fund-really-works

[11] Boccia, Romina and Rachel Greszler. 2013. "Social security trust fund reports massive deficits, benefit cuts by 2033." The Heritage Foundation. http://www.heritage.org/research/reports/2013/05/2013-social-security-trust-fund-reports-massive-deficits-benefit-cuts

12  Boccia, Romina. 2014. "How social security works in 2014." The Heritage Foundation. http://www.heritage.org/research/reports/2014/04/how-social-security-works-in-2014

13  Social Security and Medicare Boards of Trustees. 2015. "A summary of the 2015 annual reports: A message to the public." Social Security Administration. http://www.ssa.gov/oact/trsum/

14  Boccia, Romina. 2014. "How social security works in 2014." The Heritage Foundation. http://www.heritage.org/research/reports/2014/04/how-social-security-works-in-2014

15  Boccia, Romina. 2015. "Social security: $39 billion deficit in 2014, insolvent by 2035." The Heritage Foundation. http://www.heritage.org/research/reports/2015/07/sociall-security-39-billion-deficit-in-2014-insolvent-by-2035

16  Kritzer, Barbara E. 2008. "Chile's next generation pension reform." U.S. Social Security Administration Office of Retirement and Disability Policy. http://www.ssa.gov/policy/docs/ssb/v68n2p69.html

17  Rivlin, Alice M. and Paul D. Ryan. A Long-Term Plan for Medicare and Medicaid. November 17, 2010. http://budget.house.gov/News/DocumentSingle.aspx?DocumentID=225826

18  Piñera, José. 1997. "Chile's social security lesson for the U.S." Cato Institute. http://www.cato.org/publications/commentary/chiles-social-security-lesson-us

19  Brandon, Emily. 2008. "General Motors cuts healthcare for retirees." *U.S. News & World Report: Money.* http://money.usnews.com/money/blogs/planning-to-retire-2008/11/10/general-motors-cuts-healthcare-for-retirees

20  Centers for Medicare & Medicaid Services. 2015. https://www.cms.gov/

21  Allen, Elizabeth. 2015. "Why sanctuary cities must exist." Los Angeles Times. http://www.latimes.com/opinion/op-ed/la-oe-allen-sanctuary-cities-20150917-story.html

22  Ibid.

## Chapter Four

1   U.S. Energy Information Administration. 2015. "What is U.S. electricity generation by energy source?" U.S. Energy Information Administration. http://www.eia.gov/tools/faqs/faq.cfm?id=427&t=3

2   Institute for Energy Research. 2011. "Coal." Institute for Energy Research. http://instituteforenergyresearch.org/wp-content/uploads/2013/01/Energy-Inventory.pdf

3   U.S. Energy Information Administration. 2015. "Renewable energy generating capacity and generation." Eia.gov. http://www.eia.gov/beta/aeo/#/?id=16-AEO2015&region=0-0&cases=ref2015&start=2012&end=2040&f=A&linechart=~~~~~~~~~16-AEO2015.64.&map=&ctype=linechart&chartindexed=1 OR (source provided by fact checker) U.S. Energy Information Administration. 2014. "What is U.S. electricity generation by energy source?" eia.gov. http://www.eia.gov/tools/faqs/faq.dfm?id=427&t=3

4   U.S. Environmental Protection Agency. 2015. "Assessment of the potential impacts of hydraulic fracturing for oil and gas on drinking water resources." EPA External Review Executive Summary. http://www2.epa.gov/sites/production/files/2015-06/documents/hf_es_erd_jun2015.pdf

5   Institute for Energy Research. 2015. "ANWR Facts Sheet." Institute for Energy Research. http://instituteforenergyresearch.org/wp-content-uploads/2015/02/ANWR-Facts-Sheet.pdf

6   Moreno, Kasia. 2014. "Regulatory environment has more impact on business than the economy, say U.S. CEOs." *Forbes.* http://www.forbes.com/sites/forbesinsights/2014/08/12/regulatory-environment-has-more-impact-on-bsiness-than-the-economy-say-u-s-ceos/

7   Michaels, Jim. 2015. "Marines looking at deploying aboard foreign ships." *USA Today.* http://www.usatoday.com/story/news/world/2015/06/21/marines-amphibious/28935549/

8   Lunder. Erika K. and Jennifer Staman. 2012. "NFIB v. Sebelius: Constitutionality of the individual mandate." Conservative Research Service. https://www.fas.org/sgp/crs/misc/R42698.pdf

9    Homeland Security. 2015. "Deferred Action Overview." The Department of Homeland Security. http://www.dhs.gov/topic/deferred-action-overview

**Chapter Five**

1    United Press International. 2015. "U.S. interception of terrorists draws cheers." United Press International. http://www.upi.comArchives/1985/10/12US-interception-of-terrorists-draws-cheers/9532497937600/

**Chapter Seven**

1    Rove, Karl. 2012. "Karl Rove: I was wrong about Dick Cheney." The Wall Street Journal. http://www.wsj.com/articles/SB10001424052702304811304577365870484193362

**Chapter Eight**

1    Krogstad, Jens Manuel and Jeffrey S. Passel. "5 facts about illegal immigration in the U.S." Pew Research Center. http://www.pewresearch.org/fact-tank/2015/07/24/5-facts-about-illegal-immigration-in-the-u-s/

2    Hoven, Randall. 2015. "Illegal aliens murder at a much higher rate than US Citizens do". http://www.americanthinker.com/articles/2015/07/illegal_aliens_murder_at_a_much_higher_rate_than_us_citizens_do.html

3    US Government Accountability Office. 2011. "Criminal Alien Statistics: Information on incarcerations, arrests, and costs". http://www.gao.gov/assets/320/316959.pdf

4    Nuschler, Dawn. 2015. "Social Security: The Trust Funds." Congressional Research Service. https://www.fas.org/sgp/crs/misc/RL33028.pdf

5    USDebtclock.org 2015. http://www.usdebtclock.org/

**Chapter Nine**

1    U.S. Department of Commerce Bureau of Economic Analysis. 2015. "National Economic Accounts." U.S. Department of Commerce. http://www.bea.gov/national/

2    United States Department of Labor Bureau of Labor Statistics. 2015. "Labor force statistics from the current population survey." Bureau of Labor Statistics. http://www.bls.gov/cps/cps_htgm.gtm#nilf

3    Institute for Energy Research. 2011. "Coal." Institute for Energy Research. http://instituteforenergyresearch.org/wp-content/uploads/2013/01/Energy-Inventory.pdf

4    Kentucky Foundation. 2015. "10 reasons why coal is a good energy source." Kentucky Coal and Energy Education Project. http://www.coaleducation.org/q&a/10_reasons_why_coal.htm

**Chapter Ten**

1    Bureau of Economic Analysis. 2015. "News Release." U.S. Department of Commerce. http://www.bea.gov/newsreleases/national/gdp/2015/pdf/gdp1q15_adv.pdf

2    Mintel. 2014. "Americans becoming more 'self' and 'spend'-centered as consumer expenditures surpass $10 trillion for the first time" Mintel. com. http://www.mintel.com/press-centre/social-and-lifestyle/american-lifestyles-2014

3    United States Department of Agriculture. 2015. "Supplemental nutrition assistance program (SNAP)." USDA Food and Nutrition Service. http://www.fns.usda.gov/pd/supplemental-nutrition-assistance-program-snap

4    Malone, Julia. 1981. "Low-cost housing: Reagan cuts spark debate over US aid." *Christian Science Monitor.* http://www.csmonitor.com/1981/0330/033060.html

5    Kohn, David. 2002. "Tearing down Cabrini-Green." *60 Minutes.* http://www.cbsnews.com/news/tearing-down-cabrini-green-11-12-2002/

6    The White House. 2009. "News conference by President Obama, 4/04/2009." The White House. https://www.whitehouse.gov/the-press-office/news-conference-president-obama-4042009

ML    1-14